That Was Then:
A War Diary

Adolph Baker

For Dora

CONTENTS

HOW THIS BOOK CAME TO BE PUBLISHED

About ten years before his death, Adolph visited an old war friend, Saul, who lived not too far from his son Danny. In the course of their conversation, Danny discovered that Adolph and Dora had saved their old wartime letters, which were still stored in a shoebox in their home. Saul issued a warning: "Read them before it's too late, while you still have time to ask questions!" Danny nodded politely, but, like most young people, was preoccupied with other matters. About two years before Adolph's death, Danny called him up and told him he wanted to read the letters. With this as motivation, Adolph started transcribing and annotating the letters he had written home to Dora during his time in active duty, spanning the period from May 1944 to February 1945. The result is the following book.

At the time of his death in 2002, Adolph was still looking for a publisher. We have been stunned by the power of the letters to transport us back to that earlier time. Although they are precious to us as family history, we also feel they are fascinating, highly readable, and important historical documents and, as such, ought to be published. Ever since Adolph's death, it has been the intention of his children, Linda, Danny, and Ellie, to find a way to make the letters publically available. Finally, in the summer of 2012, his granddaughter Sarah (the one referred to in Adolph's Prologue as "German") agreed to go through the manuscript, edit it and put it in publishable form. The raw material for this editing was Adolph's typed manuscript. Sarah read it carefully, noting small errors and omissions. In the end, decisions had to be made concerning what to change and what to leave in its original form. Sarah's father

Danny and her Aunt Ellie went through her edits and helped make the judgment calls. Emphasis was placed on leaving the manuscript in as close to its original form as possible, although obvious typographical errors have been corrected. The word (*sic*) has been employed in several places where obvious problems exist in the text, even though it is still understandable. This word was never used by Adolph when transcribing; it is only employed by his editors afterwards. The use of "..." appears in several places in Adolph's typed manuscript, and we believe that Adolph used this to indicate places where he had omitted parts of the original letters that he deemed less interesting. These ellipses have been retained in the final version of this book.

Some readers of this manuscript have expressed surprise at Adolph's use of the nickname "Dopey" for Dora. His use of this sobriquet was jokingly affectionate and certainly not indicative of any disrespect. We have seen at least one instance in a letter of Dora's in which she addresses Adolph as "Dopey," too! The omission of Dora's letters from this manuscript has not been lost on us. Her letters, which tell another important part of the story, are still sitting in that shoe box, now residing in Ellie's attic. Given our immediate time limitations, transcribing them was beyond the scope of this project, but it is our hope that someone will, at some point, take on that project, as well. In the meantime, we can offer readers a small snippet from Dora, which was found recently in a letter dated November 22nd, 1944, that she wrote to her sister Rifka and that speaks charmingly about her relationship with Adolph at that time. She wrote:

"I got 5 letters from Adolph today...He's fine and he still loves me, thank God, because I'm mad about the guy. There are few like him in this world, and I happen to be one of the chosen lucky women to get a husband like that. I have more luck than brains or anything else – and I'm deeply grateful for the way life has treated me so far."

Although their children witnessed a much later stage of marriage, in which such arduous expressions of love were rare, we have long marveled at the underpinning of mutual respect in which they held each other for over sixty years of married life. At the time of this writing,

Dora is still alive at age 93, living in nursing care in Lexington, Massachusetts, and, sadly, has only ephemeral memories of Adolph.

At the time of his death due to sudden heart failure at age 85, Adolph was a retired Physics professor, intellectually active, and was still playing tennis, his favorite game. His children and grandchildren were extraordinarily fond of him and miss him very much.

Danny, Ellie and Linda would like to take this opportunity to thank Sarah for the enormous amount of time and energy she has devoted both to the editing process and to the work of publishing this book.

Sarah Stern
Ellie Baker
Danny Baker
Linda Baker

July, 2012

PROLOGUE

From killing Germans half a century ago, I have graduated to having a German granddaughter. She speaks English and German with equal fluency, never mixes the languages, always knowing which one to use with whom, although she will occasionally answer me in German. "Der Zeydie ist der einzige, der deutsch spricht," she says.

The letters reproduced here are a product of that earlier time, long ago. I was ordered to active duty from the Infantry Reserve shortly after Pearl Harbor, and to my surprise assigned to Recruiting and Induction in New York City's Grand Central Palace. All day long I did nothing but sign papers.

The outcome of this war was important to me, and I figured I had taken military training to be a soldier, not a pencil pusher. For someone born in these times,--when even a single American life has seemed (at least until recently) too high a price to pay in the cause of any foreign war,--it is perhaps difficult to appreciate the passions we felt then. If the enemy was to be defeated, I reasoned, it would be on the battlefield, not at Grand Central Palace. I started bombarding the Adjutant General through channels repeatedly, requesting duty with troops. But the Adjutant General must have had his mind on other things. After a year or so, just when it seemed there was no exit, a punched card dropped out of a sorter in Washington, selecting me as a linguist (in German and Russian), and I was sent to the Intelligence School at Camp Ritchie, Md.

They must have produced too many intelligence specialists, because after graduating we sat around for months doing nothing. Finally there were transfer orders away from War Dep't intelligence, sending me to troop duty with a specialty in combat intelligence.

Two weeks after D-day I was on a landing craft heading in to Utah Beach. There I was assigned as a Battalion intelligence officer in the 83rd Division, which had relieved the 101st Airborne right after their jump into Normandy. Abruptly I was immersed in total combat. Nobody was taking prisoners on either side. According to Regimental casualty figures, we were losing well over 100% per month. The expected life of a rifle platoon leader seemed to be about two weeks, and rifle company commander a month at most. The statistical probabilities were quickly apparent,---25% you would be killed and 75% wounded. If the wound was not disabling, you were returned to duty. The only rotation for an Infantryman was via body bag or permanent disability. The officer I replaced had been killed on his first day of combat.

The only way to remain sane and able to function in that environment was to accept the idea of death. I managed to survive Normandy, was hit once in Brittany, and was finally finished off in the Rhineland.

In Normandy we attacked every morning, hedgerow by hedgerow. The hedgerows had been there for hundreds of years. After the Norman invasion the farmers cut the land into small plots, and established their boundaries with mounds of earth several feet high. These became overgrown with brush, forming a natural defense barrier every two or three hundred yards. Tanks were virtually useless, since they required blasting a hole through a hedgerow to enable them to pass single file only to be picked off by antitank weapons. Infantry attempting to crawl over were pinned down by machine gun fire, and then slaughtered relentlessly by mortars and artillery which had been previously zeroed in on the same hedgerow.

At the end of the Normandy campaign, when we were motoring toward Brittany, for a day there was peaceful countryside and girls riding bicycles, and I made the psychological transition back to the world of the living. Then a few hours later it was necessary to go through the same painful reentry into the acceptance of death.

Now the terrain was more along the lines of what we had learned in the Infantry School at Fort Benning, but casualty rates remained high. The Germans were fighting with their backs to the sea. Their orders were to deny us the use of the harbors at all costs. The guns in coastline fortifications were turned around so as to fire inland, and coastal cities had to be taken one by one.

After that it seemed the worst was over, and we turned east again, chasing the enemy across France and Luxembourg, and being welcomed everywhere as conquering heroes. But after a couple of months of this nicer kind of war, we were moved to *Hürtgen* Forest, on the Siegfried Line, where there was the heaviest shelling I ever encountered. The Germans had been saving their ammunition, and now they were softening us up for their final gasp, the Battle of the Bulge. In the courtyard of a little German town called Strass the war ended for me. When the mortar barrage lifted, everyone else in the courtyard was dead, I thought both legs had been blown off at the hips, and I was sure I was dying. In fact, however, I still had my legs, having lost only one toe due to the concussion. But I had a collapsed lung, missing right shoulder joint, and a shell fragment two inches long next to my heart.

In the course of all the battles, during lulls in the fighting, I somehow managed to find time to write my wife these letters. They tell not only much of what happened during those months, but also what was said in enemy interrogations and dialogues with soldiers on both sides, in and out of combat. Annotations (in italics) fill in details I could not or would not write at the time, and comment on things I said or did then that I might not say or do now.

The story begins with a troopship on its way to England in time for the invasion of the continent, follows the war across Europe into Germany, and ends in a receiving hospital in Newport News, Virginia, where my wife and I were reunited after a year of separation. The letters sat in a shoe box forgotten for some 55 years.

Wayland, Massachusetts, Oct., 2001

1 AT SEA

Dear Dopey:

I'm on a XXXX ship of XXXX size. (Decided to do some censoring.) So far the trip has been like a pleasure cruise. The weather has been good, but in the last hour the ship has started pitching and everyone notices it. I'm afraid there'll be a bit of rail-leaner-overs, of which I sure hope I won't be one, --- if only because I would hate to have to miss any of the meals I've been getting. From point of view of service, quality, and cooking, the food is the best I've encountered in my entire Army career. Every meal is an inspiration. There are always around five courses, --- soup, fish, meat, dessert, fresh vegetables. We eat in a regular ship's dining room, and are waited upon by experienced civilian waiters. As far as the officers are concerned, except for emergency drills and uniforms, it might as well be a peacetime pleasure run. We are treated like passengers who are paying an arm and a leg to the company instead of gold bricks who are riding free for nothing.

I'm in a stateroom with five other officers. There is very little room, but it's quite comfortable. There's a window out on to the deck. You can't imagine how much money I'm saving by making the gov't pay for this trip. A large proportion of the ship's crew are waiters and orderlies whose sole purpose is to make my trip pleasant.

For the enlisted men the picture is as different as between day and night. Their food is such slop that many of them can't eat it. They sleep in hammocks three layers deep in terribly crowded rooms down in the hold of the ship. XXXX officers have always had privileges, but we've never before seen such radical distinctions made.

It was a British ship. None of this was true of the American ship I came home on a year later.

It's hard to believe that such dissimilar conditions exist on the same ship. The trip is an ordeal for the men, and a vacation for us. Our only discomfort is that we sleep with our clothes on, in deference to our Nazi chums out there under the water, and must always wear life preservers. Everybody has his own style for lugging these things around. Some carry them like musette bags, others sling them like parachutes. XXXXX ... XXX.

Spirits have been very high. During all the time we were in harbor everyone was impatient to get going. There wasn't the faintest trace of fear anywhere as we started to move out. I only heard one soldier say, "You know, I don't feel so good." Everybody was yelling and singing. Occasionally someone would try to inject a grim note by remarking, "Take a last look, Mac. It'll be a long time before you ever see that land again, --- maybe never." Then, as nobody paid any attention, "Hey, Mac! Take a last look, ... , etc."

But everyone was taking a good look anyway, just for luck, as the quiet peaceful lights of the U.S.A. grew smaller and smaller.

Once in a while you start thinking about the fact that there are people out there under the water who will kill you if they can. It occurs to you when you go to bed especially, and you prepare your life preserver and coat and canteen of water, so that you can reach them quickly. If you visualize it very much you actually do start being afraid, but it's a state of mind very easily overcome. The nurses don't show the slightest trace of fear. I don't know why this should surprise me. I don't expect the men to show it, but when women aren't afraid, it surprises me. I guess it's just male chauvinism.

2

The XXXX are exactly like they are in the movies.

The word I censored out was "British."

Sometimes I begin to suspect that moving pictures offer a realistic portrayal of life. The officers are easy to understand, but it is very difficult to make out what the waiter is saying most of the time. I generally take everything on the menu so I can't go wrong.

XXXXX way out in the distance that sounded just like XXXX, but it may have been something else.

We were in a large convoy, and one of the destroyers would drop a depth charge every once in a while.

I wonder if Josh is somewhere nearby. Wouldn't surprise me.

I won't be able to mail this till I get to the other side. I hope there'll be some letters from you when I get there.

Take it easy, baby. I am enjoying life.

Sat'y, May 6, 1944

Borrowed this ink XXXX so now my writing can last through the ages. There just isn't enough time to do anything. Eating and sleeping alone consume the best part of the day, which lasts only 23 hours (we lose an hour every day). It seems as if I no sooner finish one meal than it's about time for another. Breakfast has five courses. There's a fish plate with every meal, as well as meat.

The men are still eating slop. ("Pigs eat better," said one of them just now). Many of them are sick, --- whether because of the food or the sea I don't know.

So far the weather has been beautiful. Every morning someone opens our window, sticks his head in, and says, "Will you rise today, sir?"

They tell me it only costs $8 a day to travel first class this way in peace time. That means that for only 40 bucks or so you can take a trip to Europe for a vacation. This greatly widens my scope on the question of leisure time. I used to think that only rich people could go to Europe. So there's another one of the many things we can do after the war.

I believe we will be told today what our destination is. But everyone is pretty sure already. Of course you can always be surprised. Remember this City College boy, Sidney Schwartz, whom I mentioned in one of the letters I sent you when I was still in the States? Well, his girl friend is a nurse stationed in England. He volunteered for this overseas shipment, and his conscience bothers him, because he's not certain whether he did it to fight the war or for a chance to see his girl friend. He turned down an opportunity to go to the Pacific theatre, and is afraid that maybe he is being opportunistic. So he makes out like he doesn't care in the least where we're going. Most officers take such an individualistic attitude toward the war that I find Schwartz's desire to be a Rifle platoon leader and kill a lot of Fascists very refreshing. So I've spent a lot of time talking to him about it. His trouble is that his outlook is not a monolithic one, and his desires lack unity. He sees the war as a mission which interferes with other desires, like being with his girl, so he tries to shut his girl out of his mind. I've been trying to convince him of what you taught me, --- namely, that there is no dichotomy to be made between killing Fascists and loving women, --- that it's the same thing, and that being married doesn't make a man the worse a soldier, --- on the contrary, if he sees things in their correct relationship, it will make him a better one. Schwartz labors under the very prevalent illusion that the desire to destroy the enemy stems from pure idealism, rather than just common horse sense. And since idealists are traditionally people who sacrifice everything for their "ideal," you can see the conclusion this faulty type of thinking leads to.

However, I have gotten him to the point where he is beginning to admit that "maybe your wife has something there." But he still makes out like he doesn't care where we're going. His conscience bothers him about having turned down the opportunity to go to the Pacific theatre. He also

4

can't make up his mind whether he ought to go out with other girls or not, --- as he does, --- and is troubled over that too by his conscience.

My mind has no conflicts, and my outlook is completely harmonious. My life has been very rich and complete. I can concentrate on my work with complete tranquility. "If we were torpedoed tomorrow," I told Schwartz, "I wouldn't feel that my life has been prematurely cut off. I've had everything, have missed nothing, and would have no regrets as to my past life." He disagreed. He said he'd feel bad because he wouldn't have had a chance at the enemy first. But I meant it with regard to my past.

I can't believe all this political correctness. Soon we would be singing a different tune.

Anyway, they've got it worked out to such a system that there's about as much chance of my being torpedoed here as there is when I'm sitting in your kitchen in Brooklyn eating one of your grandma's apple pies.

Jesus Christ, it's time for dinner again. I just now finished my breakfast. More later.

Monday, May 8, 1944

After discussing security with someone I decided to cut out some of the letter. Maybe I'd better not write anymore on board altogether.

Tuesday, May 9, 1944

Am advised that love is a safe subject to write about. I love you. I love you. I love you. I love you. I love you.

The men put on a show yesterday, and broadcast it over the P.A. system. It was in the good old Schnopsy Schlickerts style. "This program is brought to you by G.I. Soap. Try crispy sudsy creamy luscious G.I. Soap today. You'll love it. In fact, it'll be the first decent meal you've had since you came on board." All their favorite peeves were aired. The five lone nurses were the subject for many a crack. When the nurses came on

5

board, said the announcer, the chief nurse asked the Captain, "Where do we eat?"

"You mess with the Officers," said the Captain.

"I know we mess with the Officers," said the nurse, "but where do we eat?"

The Captain is then reputed to have said, "I really don't know where to put you ladies. We have Officers' quarters, and enlisted men's quarters, be we have no Nurses' quarters."

"Oh, just put us anywhere," she said. "My girls can take care of themselves. You see," she added, "my girls have it up here," pointing to her forehead.

"I don't give a damn where you girls have it," said the Captain. "My boys will get it."

As it turned out, all five nurses are in the room right next to mine. You need attribute no significance to this, however, except that the hallway right outside, being the center of the ship's social activity, is always so cluttered with admirers that if we ever get torpedoed I'll be trapped.

I am trying to decide whether to get my hair cut by the ship's "Hairdresser." The sign says,

HAIRDRESSER

OFFICERS AND SERGEANTS

ONLY

If you get up enough nerve to go in, he asks you, "Will you 'ave your 'air cut, sir?" And if you say yes, he gives you an "Invayesion Special," after which your hair is definitely not as long as a music teacher's.

*Umpday, May umpteenth, 1944

*For reasons of military necessity this date must be omitted. Ed.

Dear Dopey:

A big day. Land off the starboard bow! When you've been out to sea this long land looks very mysterious and exciting. It's a beautiful day. The sun is shining in a blue sky, and the sea is sparkling. The hills out there on the horizon look like I imagine a mirage might look. They're shrouded in mist, and it's as though you can see through them to the sky beyond. I'm in my cabin sitting next to the port and I get an excellent view. Now we're passing what must be a jutting island. Its outlines are clear, --- there's no mist around it. And then ahead of it again the transparent hills.

Now it looks as if we're leaving it behind. The same regular pattern of sky, sea, and clouds. But no. If you look real hard --- maybe it's imagination --- you can see some completely transparent misty hills. They must be quite far away. I'm wearing my sun-glasses, which have come in very handy during the trip. There's no mistaking it now. At first it looked like a dark cloud, but now you can see it's more land.

It's funny. You expect land to appear gradually. But it intrudes quite suddenly. Instead of rising up from the sea slowly, there's suddenly a dim gray hulk sticking its nose way up into the air, forming a ridiculously crude design, and upsetting what was a normal picture. Now you see it and now you don't. And then it's very clear and sticks way up high into the sky. Columbus must have been a very happy guy on the first Columbus day (or is that the day he was born, I guess).

The closer we get to our destination, the warmer becomes my feeling for the people who live there. Where I always thought they were funny, they now seem very much alive and real --- and serious. Nothing really funny about being in a war. Even when you laugh about it. I hope the people like me, because I like them already. And I get sore every time I hear anyone making those silly cracks for which Americans are so famous. From now on I count those people over there as my friends, until they've given me any reasons to do otherwise.

The trip has been quite pleasant, and although it's been somewhat dull at times, at other times it wasn't so dull --- and not without some satisfactions either. I expected to do a lot of reading during the trip, but I hadn't considered the American Red Cross's evaluation of the American soldier's intellectual standards. We military men, I learned, like nothing but detective mysteries (in spite of all the letters of protest addressed to "Yank" on the quality of literature found in P.X.'s). However, one reads what one has, so for the first time in my life I concentrated my attention on that great masterpiece of modern literature, the murder mystery. However, even it is not without its interesting points.

This is the first time we've ever been separated by more than an hour or two of solar distance. I often amuse myself by figuring out exactly what you're doing. I've had my dinner today, --- but you --- you've probably just come running into your office, --- late as usual. Maybe your cheeks are nice and red --- I know they would be if you were here. The weather is nice and brisk. It's quite cold in the morning. But pleasant. In the last few days the ship has been rolling a lot. At night I roll over and back in my bunk. But it doesn't upset me in the least. I guess I've got my sea legs. After the first few days I told the Nazis to go to hell, and took my clothes off before going to bed. Why should I let them make me uncomfortable. Anyway, I can swim better without clothes.

Love from your sea-going husband, who with much tenderness sends you this, his ship's log, hoping it will in all respects please the base censor, and you as well.

2 ENGLAND

Sidney Schwartz was getting his wish. And so was I. Winston Churchill had been dragging his feet about mounting a land invasion of the European continent from the west, which Stalin had been demanding in order to take pressure off the Russian front on the east. This would have allowed the Soviet army to advance across Europe. Churchill instead figured he could destroy Germany by bombing from the air, while the German army remained bogged down in the Soviet Union. Looking over his shoulder at the Russians, in anticipation of what would come to be the cold war following the defeat of Germany, he had extended recognition to anti-Communist right wing governments in Europe, even when they were fascist, like Franco in Spain or the Mikhailovich forces in Yugoslavia,--anything to keep the Soviets from gaining control of Europe. But now it was clear to everyone that the land invasion would take place. What we did not know was the price the participants would have to pay.

Sat'y May 20, 1944 in Jolly England

Dear Dopey:

It's very rough on a guy not getting any mail, but I guess it'll catch up with me eventually. Whenever anyone gets mail around here, it comes in big batches, sometimes as high as 70 or so letters at a time.

9

I can't get over the food I'm getting here. There were two things I was told were not available on this side of the ocean --- steaks and ice cream --- and last night I had both, --- and what steak. You eat cafeteria style, so you take as much as you want. It was the very best meal I've had since I joined the Army. Everything seems plentiful here, except that eggs and milk are powdered, --- but they're quite good in that form. Of course the British don't eat all these things, and you can't get them in restaurants. My meals only cost two bits a piece, too.

I arrived at my present location yesterday, after being separated from all my chums of the boat ride and the States. My latest sidekick is called McManus --- he's part Irish and part French, and a violinist by profession, --- although at present his profession is Infantry. He's been married two months.

The camp I'm at is one of the best of its kind in the country. We're free every evening, and are located right at the edge of a town.

The town was called Chard, and it is in Somerset.

Last night I went to the "Cinema" and saw "Watch on the Rhine" again. That was really one swell picture.

I expect to visit London next Wednesday. We get a day off every week, not counting Sunday, which is free anyway. I'm really looking forward to seeing London.

There are two remarkable things about England, --- (a) the way it resembles the United States, and (b) the way it doesn't.

I still can't get over the cleanliness and orderliness. The streets are as clean as the floor of one's house. All the houses are attractive looking. So far I haven't seen any slums. The countryside, as I told you, looks just like Prospect Park. I find myself always contrasting it to Tennessee, with its dust-laden air in dry weather, and slimy mud in wet.

The people are interesting. They are much more reserved than the American people. They don't talk to strangers as a rule. But they are really quite friendly beneath it all. And the way they are so blissfully unaware of distinctions between Negro and White is even to me an endless source of amazement. I've heard a lot about race equality. But this is the first time I've actually seen it. Back in the States the few people who try to practice it do so deliberately, and nearly always with some feeling of self-consciousness. But the British people have never known anything else, --- at least as far as color distinctions are concerned. I'm not talking about economic or other differences. But so far I have seen absolutely no distinctions of any kind. That doesn't necessarily mean there aren't any. It's just that I haven't seen them. I suspect the war is breaking them down. And to me the idea that people should be no more aware of the fact that a man is a Negro than we are that he has brown eyes instead of blue is enough to make up for a lot of things. You can imagine how the white Americans feel about it. I'm sick and tired of hearing them bitching about it day and night. The favorite theme is the "injustice" of it all --- that English girls should go out with Negroes --- you can imagine all the stories that are passed around, with all the "gruesome" details.

"If it bothers you so much," I say to them, "that a girl should go out with a Negro one night and you another, you know what the solution is, don't you?"

"But how can I know which ones are doing it?" they grumble.

"You can't," I say. "But if it means so much to you, and it's a point of honor, then all you have to do is stay away from all English girls. Then you'll have nothing to worry about."

But they invariably feel that this is a rather extreme measure to take. So they just go on bitching.

The Army has gone to great lengths to warn us that it won't tolerate any funny stuff. And Negro soldiers walk down the streets so full of pride at their new-found equality that I often wonder whether they'll want to go home after the war. You can bet your boots that the lynch states are going to have a hell of a job on their hands breaking them again.

It's a very difficult subject to discuss. I always find myself standing alone in my point of view. Schwartz was the only one who ever agreed with me, and, after all, he's a City College boy, but he would never argue the point with anyone. I tell the fellows, "Well what do you expect? That's what we get for publishing the Constitution so everybody could read it . Now people all over the world think America is a democracy where everyone is born free and equal. So how can you ask them to act differently?"

Would we have fun if you could come here and visit me! You could stay in town, and I could be home every night, and walk to "work" in the morning in about three minutes. Maybe you can smuggle yourself onto a transport or something, huh? I keep getting waves of homesickness. I can be sitting in the lounge, and all of a sudden I think, "My God, I'm in England. I can't get home on a weekend. Dopey can't visit me. And it's for the duration." Anyway, England is the best place to be stationed while waiting for the fireworks to start, and I'm sure I'll have a marvelous time. One of the first things I plan to do is hear the London Philharmonic. The whole damn country is so small you can go anywhere on a 24 hour pass.

How are you, sweetheart? Since I left the States you haven't said a word, not a mumbling word.

***

Tuesday, May 22, 1944

I am living a very soft life waiting for some vacancy to occur that I can fill.

I got rather annoyed at some of the officers the other day, and did what I usually manage to refrain from doing --- allowed myself to get excited. Of course you can just imagine the sentiment on the Negro question. Back in the States you could always find somebody who believed in giving Negroes an equal chance to live like human beings --- at least theoretically ---, but over here even the most apparently enlightened individuals are shocked. The language you hear among our people is quite strong on this subject, and even to hint at any expression of sympathy for either the Negroes or the English girls who are so frequently seen walking down the street with them is to isolate yourself completely. Never have I run into such deeply rooted chauvinism. All the training Americans have received, all the movies they've seen, all the books and magazines and poolroom jokes they've been exposed to have taught them that this mixing of races is a barbarism fully as licentious as sodomy or incest. This feeling is so deep that it's like religion, --- practically useless to apply the test of logic, unless you can get one of them alone and discuss the subject quietly and impassionately, and over a long period of time. This is well nigh impossible in the Army.

But I'm getting off the subject. I've been hearing a lot of this talk, and letting it pass unchallenged for the most part, and I've been listening to more talk about the "limeys" and how if they were any good they wouldn't need us to fight their --- war for them, etc., etc. This latter point of view, of course, is not as universal, but nevertheless is a theme quite frequently played by the officers in my tent. To this I have listened also with restraint, and tried to discuss the subject seriously and dispassionately, --- and where this was not possible just let remarks go by. But after a while you just reach a point where you can no longer remain tactful. That point was reached when the selfishness of the Russian people became the topic of conversation, --- how "I'm sick and tired of hearing the Russians bellyaching about their big part in the war. Hell, they'd all be starved by now without our food. And we built all their factories and airplanes, and everything," etc., etc.

You see how the Nazi propaganda mills grind --- to foster hatreds within the nation, and between the peoples of the United Nations. So what happened? I blew up. After all, the war means so goddam much to me. It's not just a case of "when will this mess be over?" with me. You know that. Naturally, when a discussion reaches the point that one did, everyone merely proceeds to convince himself even more fully of the correctness of the position he already holds. But what the hell. A human being isn't an essay by Charles Lamb.

The last day on the boat we were oriented on this Negro situation, and the usual angry snorts and dialogue followed. I was in my cabin listening to the boys discussing it and considering where the hell I could get a word in edgewise to support the War Dep't's position on this question (which is an excellent one), and thinking, "What a hopeless muddle! How can I ever get guys who say anything like that to listen to me?"

But then a miracle took place. Before I knew it they <u>were</u> listening to me, and the discussion really progressed, and without ill feeling. I found myself getting further and further at the roots of some of the prejudices.

Finally, apparently for no reason, one of the officers said, "Look, I don't want you to feel offended, or anything ---."

"Go ahead," I said, knowing exactly what was coming. "If you're thinking it, I'd just as soon hear it. I won't be offended."

"Well," he continued. "You're a Jew. Maybe you can explain to me why it is that I've never yet seen a Jew who was broke, --- I've never seen a Jew on WPA, --- and I've never seen a Jew doing a bit of manual labor."

"You've come to the right party," I told him. "I'm really authorized to handle that question, in view of the fact that I'm usually broke, my parents were once on WPA, and my father-in-law is a bricklayer. And we're all Jews. However," I added. "If you want to know why it is that Jews have usually been in business or the professions, and so seldom engaged in the trades, there's a very good reason for it. Most Jews in this country come from Europe. And in the countries they came from Jews were not allowed to own land, and therefore couldn't farm. They weren't allowed in the labor guilds, and they couldn't be skilled artisans. The only thing they could do to live was to work as peddlers and business men, and those who came over here naturally continued to work at their original pursuits, and their children naturally were inclined to follow in their parents' footsteps. But as they become assimilated, and are getting a chance to work like anybody else in this country, they are becoming just like anybody else. However, this naturally takes time."

The guy was amazed. He had never asked this question of a Jew, but merely of some other person who would wag his head wisely and concur. So he never heard about this obvious fact. He was so impressed that he proceeded to ask me more and more questions, --- what the war was about, --- what a defeat would mean to us, --- he had been told that no matter what Germany was doing now, it was because there's a war, and once the peace comes it doesn't matter who has won. It's all the same in the end. He could see what the Jews can lose from a German victory, but, although he would do his best in the war, he frankly didn't know what he himself had to lose. He admitted that he had once been appointed Orientation Officer in his Battalion, and, not knowing how to answer the men's questions, he had had to kill a half hour every evening by merely reading the newspapers aloud to them. He had a million questions, and was visibly satisfied with the answers he got. We parted the best of friends --- he perhaps to go to one battlefield, and I to another. But I had the feeling that I had met an officer who had been destined to lead troops in a battle against Nazism while he himself hated Jews, Negroes, and all "inferior" peoples, and who hadn't the faintest notion what the war was about. And I left him if not the most enlightened of individuals, at least a man who had a new slant on things, and was not a potential victim of every tidbit of Nazi propaganda which circulates so freely among Americans, --- ranging all the way from "we'll have to fight the damned Russians in the end" arguments down to dirty jokes about Mrs. Roosevelt.

I guess in time of war every bad idea is supposed to be the result of enemy propaganda.

And then what did I do last night? I antagonized several individuals to such an extent that I hesitate even to broach the subject of politics until I've managed to make them forget the unfortunate incident, and all the righteous indignation it produced in them.

But like I said, after all a human being has emotions. He's not an essay by Charles Lamb. So long, baby face.

P.S. I still love you, you great big beautiful doll, --- like the fellers say in their letters that I have to censor. After all, how can a guy be original after reading all those letters?

But I do. No kidding.

***

Thur., May 25, 1944

Somewhere in Merrye Englande

Dear Dopey:

Just got back from my visit to London. I don't know what to tell you about first. I wish you were here. Since coming to England, in fact since I walked up the gangplank, everything has been so designed as to give me the illusion that I'm a tourist. So it seems only right that you should be travelling with me, having a good time and getting worldlier and worldlier too. But it's not that way.

Anyway, McManus and I met a young Englishman on the train named Phillipps Biggleston, who comes from Devonshire. I thought people only have names like that in books by P.G. Wodehouse, but apparently they live and breathe. Anyway, he offered to be our guide in London, and he took us all over town and kept us from getting run over by the cars that all travel on the wrong side of the street.

We really covered the town --- Piccadilly, Westminster Abbey, Buckminster Palace, the Houses of Parliament, No. 10 Downing Street, the Thames, the Prisoner of War Exhibit, and lots more.

We started at Piccadilly Station, where we came out of the tubes, and I asked P.B. in a loud voice just what Piccadilly was noted for --- I remembered it in some connection, but couldn't recall just what. Several people walking near us turned around and laughed. Apparently Piccadilly is noted not for its clowns, or its theatres, or any historical incidents. No, Piccadilly is famous for its women. And indeed, many could be seen, of all sizes and shapes and colors of hair. However, we confined ourselves to window shopping.

At Buckminster Palace your fine husband nearly caused an international incident. McManus nearly caused one the other night in the movies. At the end of all shows the British play "My Country 'tis of Thee," and everyone stands at attention. Of course they have their own words for it, but they stole the tune from us. Anyway, McManus gets up and starts to walk away, and I have to drag him back with a jerk. But my

Palace incident was even better. The British Manual of Arms is very intricate and snappy. I walked up to one of the guards, amazed at the way he was waving his arms and legs and slapping his rifle. When he was through I walked on to another guard, and he went through the same ceremony. Fascinated, I passed from one guard to another, trying to keep a straight face, when I noticed one of the guards grinning like a Cheshire cat. "What's so funny?" I asked Phillipps Biggleston. Only then did I discover that they were giving me a salute, which I failed to return. However, British-American relations have managed to survive the incident apparently.

At Downing Street we saw Winston Churchill going home after his big speech opening debate in Parliament. He looked tired and inconspicuous. The newspapers today are full of it. It was a pretty important speech, and I spent some time in the train this morning studying it. It's about the frankest exposition of current British policy I've yet encountered. The thoughts were good for the most part, but many of the papers are very critical of the treatment of the Spanish question. Although I don't concur with the vehemence of most of the criticism, there were several points I'd take issue with. He said Britain can't recognize the De Gaulle government, even as a provisional one, because he's not fully convinced that it entirely represents the French people. This is rather strange, in view of the recognition granted to some governments, notably those of Spain, Poland, and Yugoslavia. I think it's a big mistake to fool around with Spain, if it means shipping them any goods. Everyone knows Franco doesn't represent the Spanish people. Poland is of course a ticklish question, but you know what I think of the Sikorski crowd. Yugoslavia is an open and shut case. Churchill himself admits that the Mikhailovich forces have been helping the Nazis rather than fighting them, and yet he still recognizes the Yugoslav gov't-in-exile which supports and maintains Mikhailovich, instead of recognizing the Tito gov't as the only one which represents the Yugoslav people. The De Gaulle Committee is the only anti-fascist French governing body that exists today, and certainly deserves recognition as a provisional government, if King Peter and his fascist minded supporters can maintain themselves in London, as well as the Polish crowd, --- to say nothing of the friendship with Franco.

However, the speech was frank throughout, and at least Churchill is moving in the right direction, even though he hasn't completely arrived yet. The main part of his speech was excellent, and I was very pleased with it. What do you think?

Today I pulled the first duty I've had this side of the ocean --- I'm O.D. today. You know what a rough job this is. I'm all fagged out.

I'm really very pleased with the British. They're as swell as any people can be who live on an island so loaded with American troops and equipment that, as some general told us, "It's a wonder the island doesn't sink." You actually see many more American G.I.'s on the streets than you do British soldiers. The Americans have simply taken over. But I haven't yet encountered anything like the resentment of the people in Tennessee toward soldiers on maneuvers. And many English people have had to leave their homes to make way for our troops. Apparently they accept the idea of war, which our people don't. Our English friend Biggleston had a girl he was going to marry. She was killed in an air raid. These people have felt the war personally.

Listen, funny face, I still haven't gotten any mail. I'm getting so mad that I feel like blowing up the damn post office every day I'm disappointed. It makes it very hard to write. But I figure you're probably getting my mail quite regularly. I hope you've been sending yours airmail. Jesus, I'd like to see you. You little dope. I don't even know whether you're on vacation, or what. I'm fairly certain of your existence, but how can a guy be <u>sure</u> without concrete evidence? Maybe I only dreamed about you. What do you think?

So long, funny face. It's chow time. (I'm eating like a pig.)

Today I feel bored. I'm tired of being a tourist.

***

Friday, May 26, 1944

This England

Dear Dopey:

Today is the most exciting day I've had since leaving the States. My first mail arrived! Poor McManus hasn't gotten a thing, and feels very low. I'm glad it's not the other way around, or I'd be desperate. So you can imagine how wonderful I felt when the clerk handed me a neat little bundle with a string around it, consisting of 5 letters from you, and a card from my parents. The letters were dated from April 30 to May 11, and I read them like a novel, looking ahead every once in a while to make sure it wasn't coming too close to the end.

Of course it's all mixed up, and there are other letters mailed during the period which I haven't received, but now at least I know you are alive and kicking as of May 11 anyway. It was funny though, like reading a serial with some of the installments missing. I guess hereafter you'd better precede each letter with a little paragraph entitled, "What Has Happened So Far." Also a list of characters.

"DORA -- the authoress, who whenever she thinks of it writes a letter to

ADOLPH -- some zhlub she married in a weaker moment, and tells him about

JACK GROSS -- who is doing DORA's drafting for her, and whom DORA suspects of making goo-goo eyes at

ZEENA -- a mysterious woman who has been pulled out of nowheres, and has been mentioned rather casually by DORA as a potential camping trip companion.

And now to go on with the story..."

But never fear, Dopey, the other letters will catch up with me, at least 10 or 15 years after the war is over and I'm back in the States, if not sooner.

Your letters all carry an atmosphere of sunshine and green grass and pretty dresses and silver beads and all the good times we'll have when I get back, and strangely enough, paint a perfect picture of you in all that setting. I'm very glad you seem to be enjoying yourself, and getting along so well in school. I can just see you riding a bike all over Brooklyn and Prospect Park and the Parkway, and it sort of bridges the gap between us, --- because here, as I've told you, it looks like Prospect Park all over the countryside, which is a beautiful green, interspersed with multi-colored flowers of all kinds. It's just one big garden. And everyone is riding around on bikes. It isn't uncommon to see someone like your mother riding back from the grocery store with a basket in front of the bike full of groceries, or like your grandma, pedalling quietly off to *shool* on the left side of the street of a Sat'y morning, *davening* to herself.

Dopey face, I miss you so goddam much. You look so cute in your letters. You're like a little girl trying to talk like a grown-up. You don't know how smart your letters sound after the ones I have to read written by the G.I.'s. Who taught you to spell so well, anyway? Not a single mistake in all five letters. You're beautiful.

It's a good thing you don't have to see my haircut. General Eisenhower won't let me wear my hair longer than one inch anyplace.

It'll be supper time soon. My meals are my biggest contribution to the war. I spare neither myself nor the food. Nothing in the London restaurants compares with the food we get in camp. I assure you the enlisted men are not so fortunate. Indeed their lot is not a happy one. But most of them are pretty good about it, and only occasionally does one really break down in his letters and whimper. If it were up to them we'd be pounding the gates of Berlin already.

***

Sat'y, May 27, 1944

England

Dear Dopey:

McManus and I waited in front of the post office for the mail to be sorted this afternoon. After my haul of yesterday I could afford to be generous. "If only one of us gets mail," I told him honestly, "I hope it's you." There was nothing for either of us.

As we were passing the Recreation Hall we heard someone playing the violin beautifully. It was something by Wieniawski. "Come on," I said. "Let's listen."

"I don't want to," he said with a good deal of bitterness, and walked away in spite of all my urging.

I can't say I blame him. First there's the mail situation. He still hasn't gotten anything. And he's only been married two months. Then he's a professional violinist, and after spending his life studying music he hasn't touched a violin since war broke out. He's afraid of what might come out if he tried to play now. Of course my musical days are so far behind me that all the sadness is gone, but I can understand how he feels. He says he's not going back to the violin after the war. Wants to be a lawyer. Says he'll probably spend his life in relative poverty as a musician, and can make a lot of money as a lawyer. I think it's his wife's influence.

"Does she like music?" I asked him.

"Yeah, she likes music," he said. "Dance music."

He's from Nebraska, of a French mother and Irish father. He looks quite interesting, --- more French than Irish. His wife is a flower of the south --- Memphis, Tennessee. He met her while stationed down there. Looks pretty in her picture, has a private income, wealthy parents. How well I know those Southern babes.

Well, I went into the Rec. hall myself. He was really good, though far from perfection. He was practicing for a concert he's giving us

21

Sunday night. He's quite talented. I watched him play, standing there in his fatigues and leggings, looking like the usual G.I. I'd never look at him a second time if I passed him in the street, unless he failed to salute or something. But out of all that uniformity came all that individualism.

I spoke to this buck Private who makes such fine music. He comes from New York, was born in Germany and raised all over. He's 20, has studied violin since he was seven, worked under Auer and Huberman, and played under Toscanini at a music festival in Europe. He showed me a letter he had from a Special Service Company Commander, informing him of a vacancy and suggesting he apply for a transfer through channels., --- also a letter he had written to the Post Commander asking for the transfer, and the brief endorsement, "Disapproved." I informed him of his rights, and suggested that he write to the proper authorities and forward it through the Post Commander, who could disapprove it, but would have to pass it on. So we're going to see what we can do.

***

V-mail   Still Sunday, June 4

Still England

Dear Madam Dopey:

I'm writing you another V-mail letter today, on account of they are so little. Tell me what you look like, baby. Tell me what you're wearing. Tell me what you ate for dinner.

I love to torment McManus about his not having gotten any mail. "Are you sure," I ask him, "that you really married that girl before you left the States? Are you really positive that you didn't just dream it? There have been many cases," I say, "of people confusing their dream world with reality. Maybe you wanted to marry her, but never got around to it. After all, what proof have you of her existence?" He always replies with his irrefutable logic. "Go --- yourself," he says. That always holds me for a while.

You're really over there though, aren't you, dopey. I didn't just dream you, huh?

***

V-Mail   Tuesday, June 6, 1944

England

Dear Dopey:

The big news about the invasion hit us like a bang today. Only yesterday we were all sulking and growling at each other, and today we became so happy and excited that we ran around screaming at the tops of our lungs. The roar of planes overhead kept us awake last night and we lay there arguing whether or not this was It. All night long that steady roar --- and the big News this morning. I could hardly believe it --- I've waited so long. I still don't really believe it --- not till I learn how many troops and how much equipment is being thrown in. We still have no facts about it. We heard about your false alarm --- but apparently that's connected somehow to the real one. Isn't it wonderful, baby face? I wish I could call you up or something --- or at least get some news from you. Gee, I miss you so much, especially now. But if this is what it ought to be, we haven't so terribly long to wait. Almost all we can think about now is how soon we'll be kicking Nazis all the way across Europe.

***

Wed., June 7, 1944.

Still England

Dear Dopey:

Well, things really seem to be picking up for our side. Apparently we are striking at the <u>center</u> rather than the periphery of Europe, and there's every reason to believe that the news will be better and better. ... Just as surely as those G.I.'s went ploughing across the coast of France, with all those impregnable German Fortresses turned into soup by our big naval guns and aerial bombardment, --- so certain is it that before so very long I'll be sleeping with you in my arms. And any time you begin to doubt it, just think of the invasion. --- That came, didn't it? I'm certain that before long we'll be hitting them from all sides, --- from the southern coast of France, cutting off the German Armies in Italy in a second Crimea, and from the East, where the Red army will start that old offensive machine rolling again. The political phase of the war has been won already, --- because Hitler failed to split the United Nations. Now it's going to be a merry slugfest between our Armies, and those Nazi bastards haven't a chance, --- not that it'll come easy, --- but come it will.

So yesterday morning you got up, and as usual your mom probably had the radio knocking away, and came running in to wake you with the news, and you probably yelled at her, "Oh, mama, why do you always wake me up with those phoney stories!" And then you found out that it was an official announcement, and began wondering if it was really true, and becoming more and more excited, and wondering whether I was there. Or maybe your mother didn't have the radio on, and you didn't hear about it till you got into the subway and saw those headlines screaming at you. Tell me, Dopey, were the people dancing down Eastern Parkway? We were dancing all over the green when at around 0930 or 1000 yesterday morning the news got to us, spreading like wildfire. The men were lined up, and someone came running up to the Company Commander, and the Officers sensed something big, and dashed up to him. When we heard it we began hugging each other and jumping around on the Green, waving our arms and yelling like Indians. The men began shouting, "What's happened? What's happened? Please tell me, please." But we wouldn't say a word. They had to have it announced officially, with all the ceremony that the occasion deserved. And then it was their turn to start yelling. After a while they began to ask questions, "How long do you think it will take now, Lieutenant?" And everybody was wishing he was in battle already. This is how the news of the invasion was received over here.

No one was thinking about casualties, or what should have become obvious, --- that our reason for being there was to replace the bodies now lying on Omaha and Utah beaches.

24

We are simply waiting for the time when we will be assigned to regular outfits and start chasing the Nazis across Europe. Meanwhile I am continuing my study of the British People and their Habits --- for the book which I will write someday. Here are some of the results of my studies.

Most English people are women. The men seem to be away in the Armed Forces, and you see only old men and young boys around, --- but lots of women, many in uniform. England has a shortage of males anyhow, and the social habits of the country conform to this arrangement. At first the English give you the impression of being aloof and reserved, but this is only till they have broken the ice. Actually they are even more friendly and sociable than Americans, if such a thing is possible. Last night I went to a dance at a nearby town. There were a lot of women there, of all ages, and a lot of G.I.'s. At 10:30 the G.I.'s had to go home, and from then on the officers stood a chance. The dance lasted till one, and was interrupted periodically by radio broadcasts of the invasion news and the playing of "God Save the King" (really "My Country 'tis of Thee") and the Star Spangled Banner. The British girls come to a dance in dresses that you wouldn't wear while cleaning your house. They're not shabby or unclean, but of such plain style compared to the slick American eye-openers that most of our fellows figure that English girls aren't as pretty as our own. And they're not. Not only aren't they dressed well, but they carry the marks of overwork and fatigue, and perhaps not the best food. Their complexions are not good, nor are their figures streamlined. On the whole the average English girl is far less attractive than the average American girl. But she's more serious and maybe a little less affected. She has absolutely no airs, and says anything she is thinking. She doesn't consider you a wet blanket if you discuss the war at a party. To her the war is very real. Quite possibly it has already cost her a brother or sister.

Some of the social customs are very amusing. The band leader announces the nature of the next set of dances, and they begin playing a fox trot or slow waltz with that funny British rhythm that's so hard to dance to till you get used to it. At the conclusion the band leader says, "Next dahnce, please," and that means you take a break for a few minutes. The girl says, "Thenk you veddy much," and, if she thinks you're not too anxious to continue the acquaintance, promptly walks away from you.

One dance out of every three or four is called "The Ladies' Privilege." That means the girls ask the men to dance. "May I have the ladies' privilege?" they say.

Then they have an "Excuse-Me-Please" dance, which means cutting in. But the cutting in isn't done by the men --- it's the women who cut in. The first time a girl tapped me on the shoulder and said, "Excuse-me-please," I replied, "It's quite all right," and went on dancing. When I finally realized she was cutting in, I thought she wanted to dance with the other girl (girls dance together a lot here). But no. Sometimes the girls work this in teams. Just like we used to do in the old days at Benning when a group of us would arrange to corner the market on a particular girl and keep some other mob away. Anyway, I was cut in on seven times in the course of one dance, and actually didn't get to do any dancing during this period. I was amazed no end.

The British girls are very fine women, and I have a great deal of respect for them, but you kids are more to my preference, I'm afraid. Because not only would I rather be married to you, but I'd rather even dance with you, although you're not such a hot dancer, come to think of it.

It's time to eat. Jesus Christ, if only I would get some mail. I don't even know what you're thinking or doing. How do they expect me to kill Germans when I don't even know whether my wife loves me or not.

***

Friday, June 9, 1944

Fourth Day of the Invasion

England

From now on I expect to find things more and more screwed up.

That's the most consistent factor in war. My only satisfaction is the thought of how screwed up things must be in Germany, with Hitler and Goering running around with cold compresses on their heads. I believe the German people realize by now that the jig is up and it's only a matter of time. I have complete confidence in the aggressive nature of the Allied strategy, now that they have done the right thing at last. I expect thrusts from various directions soon, and the cutting up of Europe by our armies, isolating whole German armies and annihilating them in separate pockets, Russian style. I have never felt so optimistic since I first took an interest in political events. Every once in a while I pinch myself to make sure it's true --- it's so wonderful. I can't believe it. The relative absence of German air forces is significant, I think. Of course they are saving their power, but everybody holds out reserves, and the fact that we hold a 200 to 1 air superiority over beachheads is a very good sign that the Nazis are short. There are now too many fronts, too many enemies, and Hitler is a tired old man. This war has been so full of surprises, and one must always expect the worst, but why not enjoy oneself when things look good at last. If it is true that the Nazis might still surprise us, and the war last a long time, it is also true that they might collapse sooner than in our wildest dreams, and personally I am more inclined to believe that. But I'm ready for anything. The biggest thing about it all is that the phoney old myth about impregnable fortifications will never be trotted out again to hold us up. We have the men and the equipment. Nothing can stop us now. I know you're as excited as I am, and I sure do intend to see the Statue of Liberty again and to see the look in your eyes when I run up the steps and hold you so tight that nothing will ever separate us again. But of course there are certain things that must be done first.

**

Monday, June 12, 1944

England

Dear Dopey:

For the first time since crossing the big pond I went swimming today. It was so cold it hurt, but it was swell. The whole Company went -

-- officers and men --- we spent the afternoon gambolling on the green and splashing around in the lake. The men's morale soared 600%. Everyone felt clean and healthy. Then a detail of men went to a nearby cider mill and got a dozen or so cases of Champagne Cider (a very popular drink in these parts --- mildly alcoholic), and we guzzled it until our stomachs were bloated. I suppose all the men will be writing home about it just as I am. Relations between officers and men are somewhat different over here from what they were back home. There is less strict formality, and they all play ball together (Officers always lose) and kid around and compare gripes to an extent which would be somewhat abnormal back in the States. One of the officers after playing a game with the men had to run the mill while the men whacked at him with their belts, and he had such nice juicy welts that his rear end bled --- all in good spirit, I assure you. The English are amazed at the way we kid around with the men --- such a thing is unheard of in the British Army. Actually, in spite of the relaxing of some of the formalities, discipline is better. Very rarely do you pass a soldier who fails to salute. The men look to their officers for guidance in everything. I hear that this increases the closer you get to combat. An officer means a lot to them. They know that the junior officers take greater risks than their men, and they respect (but seldom envy) them, and instinctively turn to them for leadership. The relationship is a very good one. I can tell that the men like us. You can see the way they act. Their letters show it. Where men in the States resent some of the privileges officers have, here it seems more natural (for one thing there are fewer privileges) and the men accept it. You see, a soldier should be as near to the fighting as possible if he's to be a good soldier. Otherwise many things seem ridiculous. I don't know how things will be when I get assigned to my permanent outfit, but I hope it will be the same. I am very glad I'm an officer --- and I mean a <u>combat</u> officer. We have open contempt here for what we call the "Button boys" --- the swivel-chair officers. (Yes, there are plenty of them here too), and for all I'll have to go through, I want nothing better until we (I'll be proud that I will really be able to say "we") have finished the war.

***

I remember our life together so clearly that it's almost the real thing. That's one thing they can never take away from me. No matter what happens I can recreate you in my mind any time I like. It's wonderful to have something like you inside a guy. And when I think of combat the only thing that really worries me is that I'll do something that would make you ashamed of me. By some rather obtuse mathematical computations I have definitely established the fact of my survival at the end of the war, and this doesn't worry me too much. But I'm so anxious to do well and be the kind of officer you deserve to have for a husband (and I know that I'm not), that all my failings, both personal and those due to improper training, worry me. I suppose that no matter how much a man is trained he is never really prepared for combat. The main thing is guts and a consciousness of what it's all about. I know I have the second requirement. But the first is yet to be established. Whatever happens, I'll always be seeing you, all white and shiney and dewey looking. You absolutely gleam. If you knew how clearly I can see you it would make you blush. I'm afraid there is very little if any clothing in the picture. I can't even remember what your clothes look like. I do remember that you did wear them.

***

June 15, 1944

Dear dopey darling:

It's a month today since you wrote the last letter I've received from you --- a gap of a whole month during which anything in the world might have happened to you. I don't even know if you're alive. I was so angry today after getting no mail again that I walked around for two hours uttering the most obscene rantings I've ever been guilty of.

Did I tell you the story about the soldier who hadn't heard from his wife for a whole year? He got so disgusted that he wrote her a letter telling her to go to hell and file a suit for divorce. The day after he mailed that he got 300 letters from her. He got special dispensation from the War Dep't to burn up the wires with cabled explanations. Or so the story goes.

You do still love me, don't you? After all, how do I know? People change. The way guys always ran after you --- maybe some 4F or Air Corps pilot or button boy or somebody finally showed you how dopey you were for ever falling for me in the first place.

***

Nothing a woman does is really wrong, no matter how much suffering she causes a guy. It's just life.

3 UTAH BEACH – *STE.-MÉRE-EGLISE*

If God was on our side, He certainly was not showing it weather wise. First the invasion had to be launched under unfavorable conditions, and then replacements were held up in a storm in the Channel for a good part of a week, unable to land. Finally on June 22 the weather improved, and landing craft pulled alongside our ship. We descended rope ladders into an LCT (Landing Craft Tank), where two or three hundred men of my Replacement Unit were packed with all their weapons and field equipment. When we reached land they dropped the front end to unload us. But the tide in that part of Normandy comes in so fast that before we could get everyone on to the beach the water was suddenly too deep. From nowhere the amphibian "ducks" appeared and carried us all to shore. It had been named Utah Beach. The first French town I remember was Ste.-Mére-Eglise.

While I was landing at Utah, the 83rd Infantry Division was being put ashore several miles to the east at Omaha Beach. From there they would move south of Carentan to relieve the 101st Airborne, which had jumped in the neighborhood of Ste.-Mére-Eglise the night before D-day. In the hedgerow fighting that followed, the 83rd would take heavy losses. Among the first to die would be a Lieutenant Michael, of the 2nd Battalion, 330th Infantry Regiment. He would be replaced by me,-- just as I

in turn would be replaced by someone else when my time came.
We were all expendable. That was the way it was.

Friday, June 23, 1944

Somewhere in France

Dear Dopey:

I don't know just how to begin this letter--there are a million thoughts running through my mind. When I jumped out of the landing craft and ran up the beach, the first thing I thought of was you, and I scooped up a handful of sand and let it run through my fingers, and I remembered how long you and I have waited for this. This field and everything around it were hopelessly Nazi only a few days ago, --- and now the only Nazis are the endless streams of prisoners moving down toward the beach. Hitler's boys must have been pretty hard up for men to man these impregnable fortifications, from the looks of the prisoners, who represent the nationalities of every occupied country in Europe. Things move pretty fast around here. After all these fruitless years of searching for it, I've finally found the efficiency that the Army has been so short of. There's no red tape over here. Everybody just helps everybody else. I suppose I should withhold judgment for a while, though. I've got a lot to learn. I've learned to appreciate three things already, --- the Air Corps, the Seabees, and the Ducks, or amphibian 2 1/2 ton trucks, --- most of all the Air Corps. You must have read of the troops and supplies held up for days in the English Channel because the sea was so rough that it was impossible to land on the beach. We lay out there till we were out of food, out of water, out of fuel. We were just clay pigeons for the invincible *Luftwaffe*. But not a single German plane dared to come and get us. And even here they only dare to come out at night. That, baby, is known as air superiority.

We arrived in this area at night, and went stumbling around looking for a hole to crawl into for the night. The first big difference from maneuvers I discovered was that you never sleep at ground level. My left hand is nice and juicy with several great big blisters I worked up while improving my temporary home. Because of air bombings and long range artillery fire you always dig in before going to sleep. Anyway, when we arrived we found a lot of individual slit trenches, but they were full of tin cans (incidentally, everything I've eaten since leaving England has been out of tin cans). The slit trenches looked very unappetizing, and I said to McManus, "I wonder if we can't find something more commodious." I finally located a somewhat larger trench which we promptly converted into a 4-man suite. McManus, McKee, and Marchik, --- these are the men with whom I spent my first night in France.

When we were finally bedded down, we lay there batting the breeze and thinking and listening to the noises of battle. Usually this rumble came from the front lines some miles away, but occasionally it would be close enough to make us hold on to our helmets and hug the ground. "It's a long way we've come," I said to them, "and here we are in the same slit trench --- two Irishmen and two Jews."

"You know something," said McManus. "It smells awful funny in here."

"I was thinking the same thing," I said. "You don't think ---?"

"It is funny that such a nice trench should have nobody already sleeping in it," said McKee.

"Still," I said, "if it was, we would have noticed it when we got in. It sure does smell like it though."

"I tell you what," said McManus. "This could be the home of some animal --- a skunk, for instance?"

"You know what?" I said. "Whatever this hole is, we'll smell a helluva lot worse before many days are over. So let's just go to sleep." Which we did.

It's amazing how, with the bloody thing war is, the civilians remain. Yesterday the Germans were here, today the Americans, tomorrow maybe somebody else, and yet these people go right on, calmly leading their sleek handsome looking cows to pasture. *"Comment ce vas?"* we yell over to them, and they turn around and smile, *"Tres bien, tres bien!"*

You should have seen the spectacle a few minutes ago of some G.I.'s talking to a little French boy, holding the French phrase books in one hand, and gesticulating wildly with the other. The little boy was wearing an immense pair of G.I. shoes, and holding a puke sack full of candy. (We were all issued vomiting bags, familiarly known as puke sacks, before crossing the Channel. A lot of the boys were terribly sick all the way). Anyway, here was this little boy with the big shoes and puke sack, talking beautiful fluent French. And only a couple of days ago it was Cockney English we were listening to.

We became very chummy with the British sailors on the trip over. They had taken part in the D-day assault, and were as swell a bunch of guys as you could find anywhere. There wasn't a thing they wouldn't do for us. It's funny how all the anti-British talk about the damned limeys vanishes when the shooting starts. Everybody gives everyone else the shirt off his back. This one British sailor I got to know piloted a landing craft on D-day, and when his boat was hit he was fished out of the water by an American ship. He couldn't stop talking about the chicken dinner they fed him. "Blimey," he said. "I ain't had no bloody chicken since the --- war began." He said they'd all join the American Navy tomorrow if they could. It's the same everywhere. People look to America as the land of miracles --- Hollywood movies, and chicken dinners, and streamlined cars.

Sat'y, June 24, 1944

Somewhere in France

Dear Dopey:

In the letter I wrote you yesterday I told you about the three fellows who share my trench with me. Well, there are only two now. McManus moved up to the front last night. At one in the morning someone woke him up, and in ten minutes he was gone. I miss him. We became sort of chummy during the month I spent with him. And then suddenly he's up and gone. I got up, helped him pack, and saw him off. We didn't know

34

what to say. He said, "Good luck," and I said, "Take it easy." That was all. I hope I run into him again.

Of course I never did.

This afternoon I took a walk to a nearby battlefield. You could see the whole story as you walked down the trail. First the parachute harnesses where our paratroopers landed, parachutes and equipment strewn all around --- then, further on, where they met the Germans. The Nazis must have been having chow. There was mess equipment all over the place, German gas masks, bloody German gray-green uniforms, and broken rifle butts. Further on you came to an unusual shell crater, big enough to have been made by a block-buster, and alongside it the ruins of a big French chateau, which must have been German headquarters for this area. There were official documents and field orders all over the floors and tables, and interrupted letters. We went out of the chateau, and then came to the end of the story. There was a sign, "Kangaroo Cemetery." I don't know why it had that name. There was an arrow pointing left that said, "American," and right that said, "Enemy." Among our graves was one of a Brigadier General who was the Assistant Division Commander of the Airborne Division which apparently had the mission, among other things, of destroying the German command post, and must have done a good job of it. The General was killed when his glider crashed. The wreckage was several hundred yards away.

***

Sunday, June 25, 1944

Somewhere in France

Dear Dopey:

I threw away some more equipment yesterday. When I finished maneuvers back home I made myself two promises --- (a) to travel light, and (b) always carry toilet paper in my helmet. I never forgot about the toilet paper, and many an embarrassing moment it has saved me. But it's very hard to resist the temptation to carry around everything but the kitchen sink in one's bedding roll. The U.S. Army Officer's Bedding Roll holds an infinite amount of equipment, and it just gets bigger and heavier the more stuff you put in it. It wouldn't be so bad if everything was an essential item, like you for instance. I wouldn't mind carrying you around in my bedding roll. But you never see the damn roll up on the front lines if you're an Infantryman, and every time you move somewhere you have to drag it down to some truck around a quarter of a mile away. And orderly service is very lacking in the combat zone. So I've whittled my roll down to a neat little job of about 15 inches in diameter by 30 inches long, and it has only my sleeping bag, two blankets, some changes of socks, handkerchiefs, underwear, a tent, an extra pair of G.I. shoes, tent poles and pins, some sterno soap, my overcoat, and a few other little odds and ends. Now at least I can pick it up off the ground and throw it over my shoulder without breaking my back. I'll probably never see it again once I get to the front lines. All you carry there is weapons, ammunition, water, concentrated food, a shovel, and a gas mask, --- and, if necessary, you can always throw away everything but weapons and ammo.

In fact, before going into combat we threw away the gas masks.

I kept thinking about you all night last night.

***

The Army does such funny things sometimes, like issuing rubber contraceptives to everyone before we left England. Nobody knows what to do with them, so they blew them up like balloons. We also used them during the landing to keep salt spray from getting into our weapons.

I just ate dinner --- the usual "C" ration --- a can of meat and vegetable stew, lemonade made of lemon powder and water, candy, and crackers (You always throw away the crackers). The meat and vegetable stew was delicious. It gets to taste like roast chicken after you've gone hungry awhile (as we did in the Channel while waiting several days for the sea to calm down so we could land on the beach).

***

Monday, June 26, 1944

Dear Dopey:

Imagine what happened today --- mail! Two stinky little V-mail letters from you, but still, mail. I had forsaken all hope of ever hearing from you again. I had resigned myself to having to wait till the war ends, and was making up letters that you might be writing to me. It's not so remarkable to live in a dream world as far as you people back home are concerned. The whole idea of war is like some dream anyway. I still can't believe it. Last night there was a lot of excitement, but I slept through the whole thing. Unless the action gets very close, a slit trench offers such wonderful protection that I feel as safe as if I were home in bed with you. However, the similarity ends there. Anyway, there'll be plenty of time to stay awake when I'm up in the front lines. War isn't really quite as dangerous as people make out, anyway. Marchik was saying to me this morning as we lounged in our luxurious slit trench, "You know, actually, they tell me you're safer here than you are in New York."

"Who's afraid of risks?" I said. "I'll take New York."

"This is how I see the mail situation," I tell the guys. "The letters go following you all over England, see? Then you come here, and just when they're about to catch up with you, you get shot up and they have to send you back to England for a repair job. The letters follow you back to England, and just about that time you're fit for duty again, and they send you back to France. The same thing happens again, and the letters go zigging and zagging back and forth that way, until suddenly one day by coincidence you and the mail happen to be in the same place at the same time. Then you get around 600 letters, see? And they have to give you a 30 day leave to read your mail."

"30 days?" somebody says. "Where'd you ever hear that?"

"It's right there in regulations," I say. "Read it for yourself. It's only logical," I add. "That means you read 20 letters a day. It just gives you time to read and answer them all."

"I never heard about that," they say.

37

"Look it up in regulations," I tell them.

***

I just had another delicious dinner of "C" rations. I can't understand it. Instead of getting tired of it, I enjoy it more every day. They heat up the cans in boiling water before distributing them, and it tastes very good. No kidding. We eat it right out of the can. We never use our mess kits, since there's no water available for washing them. It's drizzling outside, but I'm nice and cozy in my slit trench, with my tent set up over it to keep the rain out.

In comparing dates I notice that your Calculus exam came out on D-day. Must have made it pretty damn hard to study, if you were as excited as I was.

***

Tuesday, June 27, 1944

Dear Dopey:

I went down to the local evacuation hospital last night to talk to a Russian prisoner who I had heard works there. He turned out to be an Uzbek, 27 years old, with a wife and four kids back home. There is no one else in the vicinity who knows Russian, and he has nobody to talk to. I had no trouble at all conversing with him. I was surprised myself at how easy it was for me. And so he told me his sad story. This is it:

He was captured on the Russian front, Kursk sector, last July. He was a medic, but because of heavy casualties among combat troops he was assigned to the Infantry as a messenger. It was in this capacity that he was captured by the Germans. He told me a gruelling story of starvation in German prison camps, and of thousands, probably millions, of people sent back to Germany in slavery to work for the Nazis. He was in a prison camp for 10 months, and was then packed into a train and told he was being sent somewhere to work. Before he knew what had happened he was a horseholder in the German Army. They never gave him a gun, but it was his job to groom horses, wash them, and lead them around. Shortly afterward his horse fell, killed by an American bullet, the Germans withdrew, and he dropped to the ground, mortar fire bursting all around him. When the American soldiers came up he jumped to his feet and surrendered himself. He said there were 15 or 16 Russians like himself in his company, as well as in the other companies of his Battalion. There were many Poles, and men from all the occupied countries. He said there were actually only around 90 Germans in his company -- a German Rifle Company has 185 men, so figure it out for yourself.

He said he is well treated here, gets plenty to eat, but of course is very anxious to get home. He was hungry for news about the Russian front, --- said he's heard practically no news for a year --- there's no one here who can talk to him. Although he looks like a typical Uzbek, he seemed to me to speak fairly good Russian, and had the typical Russian characteristics --- a warm smile, and the usual Russian sense of humor.

Those poor crumby Nazis must be in a pretty sad state to have to resort to this sort of thing. The fellows wanted me to talk to some of the German prisoners who were working at the hospital, but I didn't feel like it, --- I felt so much like emptying my gun into every one of them that I figured it was best that I shouldn't start a conversation there. I figure there's no point in kicking a man when he's down -- I'll get my chance to talk to them in the language they know best soon enough.

Today I began my study of the French language. The way it happened was that I went to a nearby farmhouse to take a bath at a well. A French farmhouse isn't at all like the American version. It's built of stone, and has stone walls around it instead of a fence. I drew some water into my helmet, and started to sponge myself from head to foot. Women would pass nearby occasionally, but they never even turned their heads -- - I guess if they weren't embarrassed, there's no reason why I should be. The only one who took any interest was a pretty little girl who was wearing a G.I. Infantryman's garrison cap. She sat in a swing and rocked back and forth laughing at me. Her name turned out to be Marie, and she is seven years old. I began calling her *mon ami* from the moment she pointed at my trench knife, and said, *"Couteau --- pour les Boches,"* and moved her finger across the front of her throat in a cutting motion. So our laborious conversation began --- and my French lessons. *"Qu'est-ce que c'est,"* (disregard the spelling), I would say, pointing at my carbine. *"Fusil,"* she replied. Water, --- *d'leau.* Knife --- *couteau.* Watch --- *l' mond.* Underwear --- *chemise.* She has two brothers and two sisters, and her mother and father. Her father passed by, carrying a big scythe. He swung it through the air, smiled at me, and said also, *"Pour les Boches!"* I said, *"Oui."*

Oh, I forgot to tell you something about the Russian. I asked him how he likes the Soviet government. He said, "Very much," and told me that life was very good for them before the war.

He had the same reserved modest way of speaking that Valya has, and reminded me very much of her--although he was apparently not as educated--he was a chauffeur before the war.

> *I wish I had thought to ask him about the Moscow trials. During the thirties virtually the entire original leadership of the Communist Party, (anyone who might ever become a rival to Stalin) was arrested and charged with being traitors and agents of a foreign government. They proceeded to "confess" in open court, and all were executed. The wagons my mother told me about that carried the condemned to the execution grounds had been rolling again. But this time the Revolution was devouring its own children. However, I never thought to ask what he thought about all this. My mind was on other things.*

McKee just came back from a stay at a hospital. He said one of the German wounded they brought in was scared to death of the hospital. He was a young kid, and said he had been told that the Americans castrate all prisoners.

Last night we had a heavy rain, and had to keep bailing out our slit trench. Today we worked on it, making big improvements, using our tents over the top. It's so fancy now it'll be a pity to leave it. It even has a guest room --- everything but hot and cold running water. Well, last night we had cold running water.

I hear we've finally cleaned up Cherbourg. Now watch our smoke, dopey.

***

Wednesday, June 28, 1944

Dear Dopey:

I went over to the hospital to see the Russian prisoner again last night. I brought him a copy of Stars and Stripes, with a map of the Russian front. I never intended to talk to the German prisoners, but as soon as I got out the map they crowded around and started asking questions. "Shmolensk, Shmolensk," one of them began to jabber, pointing it out on the map, and rolled up his sleeves to show me his wounds. "Wounded twice --- Shmolensk," he said, holding up two fingers. "Rzhev," said another one. "Five times," holding up all the fingers of one hand. As soon as they saw I could speak German, they all crowded around, asking questions. I told them about the Red Army's advances, and that we had just taken Cherbourg. "But the Germans fought to the last, didn't they?" one of them said.

"They fought," I said. "But it did them no good."

"The Germans will fight until the last German soldier is gone," he said.

"From the looks of things," I told him, "they're fighting not only to the last German soldier, but to the last Russian and Pole," and I pointed to the Russian and Polish prisoners. "Tell me something," I said. "Do you think the Germans have a chance of winning the war?"

"The Germans will fight to the end," he repeated like a phonograph record.

"*Sie beantworten meine Frage nicht,*" I said. "You're not answering my question. Do the Germans have a chance of winning?"

He smiled sadly, dropped his eyes, and said quietly, "Against the Americans --- no."

"And against the Russians?" I said.

"No."

"Does the rest of the Army realize this?" I asked.

"Everyone knows it now," he said. "The officers stand behind us with pistols, and when we put up our hands to surrender, they shoot us. Many of my friends were killed in this way. But whenever we can we give ourselves up."

"What do you think of Hitler?" I asked. My friends who were with me kept putting questions to me to translate to the Germans.

"At first we thought he was very good for the country --- making a better life for us. It would have been good if he had stopped at the beginning. But how can Germany fight the whole world?"

"Didn't you realize," I said, "that you'd find yourself fighting the whole world?"

"If Hitler had stopped at the right time," he said, "everything would have been all right. But there's something wrong with him," he added, pointing with his finger to his forehead.

"Do the rest of the people think as you do?"

"Yes."

"Don't they realize," I asked, "that they'll have to pay for the crimes of the Nazis?"

"We can do nothing," he said. "Revolution in Germany is impossible. Everyone who opposed Hitler has been killed. Everywhere there are guards. Hitler is so closely guarded no one can get near him. In the Army the officers stand behind us with pistols. There can never be a revolution in Germany."

I asked him about Hess, repeating a question one of the fellows wanted me to ask him.

"Hess didn't agree with Hitler," he said.

"What was the disagreement?"

"He wanted to make peace with England," he said. "He thought Hitler was taking on too much."

"Whom would you rather fight?" I asked. "The Russians or the Americans?"

"Oh --- the Americans," they all said. "We'd rather not fight anybody, but as long as you have to be a soldier, we'd rather fight against the Americans."

"Why?" I asked.

"The Russians are terrible," he said. "They are very brutal. They torture prisoners --- cut off their ears, and put out their eyes."

I thought of the young German kid McKee had seen, who was so afraid of hospitals, because his Sergeant had told him that Americans castrate their prisoners.

"He says the Russians torture prisoners," I said to the Russian. "Have you ever seen this?"

"Never," he said. "Why should we torture them? We kill them -- that's all."

I turned back to the Germans. "You know why the Russians hate you so much? You've destroyed their homes, murdered their women and children."

"The SS did it," said one of them. "When I was at the front, it was quiet, we never got to any cities. The Nazis did all those things --- the SS divisions."

"Do you mean to say," I asked, "that only the SS committed those atrocities? --- that the ordinary German soldier was never guilty?"

"There were others," said another prisoner. "There was the Green Mountain Division." (I believe that's the name he gave. I don't remember it exactly.) "The Russians dropped leaflets over them, informing them that because of what the men of this Division had done, not one would be spared. And so it was. The division was completely wiped out. Not a man was left alive."

"Do you know," I said, "that the Germans have murdered two million Jews in Poland and Russia, not only men, but women and children?"

"Yes," he said. "I know."

Marchik wanted me to ask them how they did it. "Is it true," I said, "that many of these Jews were killed with gas?"

"None that I know of," he said. "All I ever saw were shot through the head."

"What do you think of the Jews?" I asked the most brutal looking of the bunch. He had absolutely the most depraved face I have ever seen. I figured that in the course of his military career he must have raped some dozen women, and smashed many a baby's head against a stone wall. But of course faces can be deceiving.

"I have nothing against the Jews," he answered in a thick Low German accent. I found it hard to understand him. "The rich men back home making money from this war are worse than any Jews I have ever known."

"The way I see it," said another, "is that there are good Jews and bad ones, just the same as with any other people. Before Hitler the Jews did many good things for Germany."

I couldn't get one of these supermen to express even the faintest hint of anti-Semitism. I then told them that I was a Jew, to see if springing this on them would make them change their tone toward me. But there was no change --- only an interest that in the American Army a Jew could be an *Oberleutnant*.

"We are very happy here," they all said, when I asked them how they are treated here. "Never in many years have we eaten so well." Then with a sly grin, "Our soldiers know how well the Americans treat their prisoners."

"Then you wouldn't like to go back to Germany?" I asked.

"After the war, yes. I want to go home to my family --- but not till after the war."

"Would you like to go home?" I asked the Russian, "and be sent back to the front to fight again?"

"But of course," he said. "What a question!"

> *One of the things I learned in the following months is that prisoners do not necessarily tell you exactly what is on their minds; they may be telling you what they think you want to hear. On the other hand, I came to know American soldiers also who wanted to return to their outfits after being wounded and evacuated. But the Red Army men were a whole other thing. They were said to charge against the enemy shouting, "Za rodinu! Za Stalina! For the motherland! For Stalin!" It is hard to imagine American G.I.s charging to their death shouting, "For Roosevelt!" or "For Johnson!" or "For Nixon!"*

It was getting late, and I wanted to talk to the Russian some more, but a couple of the Germans kept hanging around. The Russian could speak only Russian, and the Germans only German, and they were hungry for conversation.

"You know," said the little German who had done most of the talking, when I asked him why the Germans had supported Hitler in the beginning and for so long. "It's not our fault. All we ever got was propaganda. We heard only what the Nazis told us. "Do you know," he said confidentially, "that in Germany you're not allowed to listen to foreign broadcasts on the radio?"

"I know," I said. "We know a lot more about Germany than you do about us."

"Of course," he said. "We never even knew what was happening in the world. We were told only what Hitler wanted us to know."

"You won't get any sympathy from me," I said. "First of all I'm an American. In the second place I'm Russian." I counted the points off on my fingers. "And in the third place I'm a Jew. You understand?"

"I understand," he said.

"And since, as you say, the Germans will fight to the end, I will kill many Germans. You know that, don't you?"

"Yes," he said. "I know."

"Gute Nacht," I said.

"Gute Nacht," he replied sadly, and walked away.

The Russian remained behind, and a Polish prisoner some of the fellows had been trying to talk to in broken French. The Pole started to leave, and said in what must have been a mixture of Polish and Russian, "Hey, Ivan, come on." The Russian said, "I'll come later."

"What's your hurry?" said the Russian. "The night is long."

So I remained behind to talk some more. I got a lot of information from the Russian.

"Are these Germans around here typical of the German Army?" I asked him. "Everyone suspects that the Germans are holding their best troops in reserve. When you were in Germany, did you see many tall healthy ones, or were they all little ones like these?"

"Everywhere," he said, "it's the same. Most of the best ones are dead. All you see is men like these, in their forties. And look how they use us, and Poles, and Czechs." He told me that they use the Poles and others as regular soldiers, just like the Germans, but they never arm the

Russians. They use them in the non-combatant services. The Germans had told me this too, when I told them they must be pretty hard up for troops. Only one of the Germans said it was voluntary, and the Russian said he was a damned liar.

Oh, yes, I forgot to tell you that the Germans told me that when they would come home on leave from the Russian front, they'd tell their wives that they had gotten it fixed up so they could be transferred to the *Afrika* Corps, and that as soon as they got to Africa they would give themselves up. They said that nothing was ever heard from those lucky ones and it was presumed by their families that they had succeeded in getting themselves captured.

I asked the Uzbek many questions about the Red Army. He said that discipline is very strict, but that off duty the officers and men go to the same dances and social affairs, but that saluting is maintained everywheres, even in combat, except when actually firing a gun. (I haven't seen a single man salute over here since I landed in France.) He said that the officers' training in the Red Army is very elaborate.

I learned two things about my so-called linguistic abilities, --- namely, that my Russian is much better than I thought, and my German much worse. I conversed with the Russian with ease, but often had to ask the Germans to explain themselves. Some Germans were much easier for me to understand than others. But I know now that all I need is practice in both languages. I found myself getting all confused when I tried to maintain a three-way conversation in Russian, English, and German. When I would switch from Russian to German, I'd find myself using Russian words when I would try to think of the German. It's particularly confusing, since I've been trying to pick up as much French as possible. But I was really amazed at how easily the Russian came to me.

These, dopey, are the latest adventures of your travelling husband. If I keep learning new things at the rate I have been, I'm going to write a book, or ten books, or something.

***

Tuesday, July 4, 1944

France

Dear Dopey:

This is the first 4th of July I've ever spent in which fireworks would be quite superfluous, and I hope it'll be the last. Our artillery celebrates the fourth of July every day of the year, and whenever they lay down one of those Hitler specials, it sounds like the end of the world. You can't even hear the individual charges --- just a continuous roar. The other night McKee woke me up. "Hey, get up," he said. "Listen to that!" I couldn't help listening. It sounded like Niagara Falls, the Russian Revolution, and Paulie when she gets mad at something, all rolled into one. There wasn't the faintest chance of being able to go back to sleep with that going on.

"What'd you wake me up for?" I asked McKee.

"I figured you'd want to hear it."

"Don't you think I ever heard an artillery barrage before?"

"Sure," he said. "But I figured a barrage like that would make history, and I know you wouldn't want to miss anything that would make history."

"Listen," I told him. "I never did like history. When I was in high school I nearly flunked history. I never could remember the dates. And although, personally I've got nothing against history now, I sure as hell don't intend to lose any sleep over it, unless I'm making it myself!" I had to yell to make him hear me over the noise.

At a time like that it's always a good feeling to be below ground level, in a nice hole, where you can lie flat on your stomach and press your helmet to your head like a derby hat. After all, the Germans have artillery too. It's really swell, though, to be on the winning side. The Nazi Infantry must feel pretty wistful when our Artillery opens up. I can just picture them crouching low in their foxholes and cursing the day they

48

ever said, "Heil Hitler." The poor *Luftwaffe* provides the saddest picture of all. Those brave Nazi falcons are afraid to leave the ground. I'm learning a lot about aircraft identification, but only with respect to Allied planes. Honest, I haven't seen one German plane since I landed in France. The fellows say the Germans have a new system of aircraft identification. If it's three or more planes, they're Allied --- shoot at them.

I gave some blood to the local hospital today. I figure that after all the money I've collected from the government I ought to do something for the war effort.

***

I talked with some of the wounded who had just been brought back. They all have the same quiet subdued way of talking, and tell what happened to them just as you might discuss the day's events in your office. One radio operator was very upset about the fact that his radio had been smashed. "I was dug in," he said, "and I was trying to get the radio dug in, and their mortars started bracketing in on me. When they hit me, the radio was right up in the open, and it was completely wrecked. They won't even be able to fix it," he moaned. "Oh, God, if only I had the radio dug in."

***

Thursday, July 6, 1944

France

Dear Dopey:

Three big things happened yesterday --- my two remaining trenchmates, McKee and Marchik, moved out, we had real bread for supper, and I received mail from home. I left our area early yesterday morning with a couple of hundred men on a detail, and when I got back in the evening, I found that I was all alone in that nice big slit trench, which we all worked so hard to make comfortable. Now I'm alone. It's always like that with me. Fate is so slow in handling my case.

Our food is getting so fancy now --- we eat out of mess kits instead of cans, and as I said, we had real fresh bread for supper yesterday. But the big surprise was the mail. I had begun to despair of that. I see that you were assured that I was getting your mail all right, just as they told us that you were getting ours. So we were both fooled. But of course we know now that it was because of the invasion, and I hope it will start coming through pretty smoothly from now on. ...

When you get to the combat zone everything is free. One guy is sending home a German machine gun, piece by piece. I'd like to get hold of a Luger pistol and a pair of German field glasses. Most of the men pick these things up on the battlefields. There's certainly plenty of it. But you'll never catch me getting anything that way. I try to remember everything I've learned, and the most repeated warning is --- don't go around picking up things. The Germans know everybody wants a Luger and they love to booby trap them. No matter how many times you warn a man about booby traps, every American is such an inveterate souvenir hunter that he won't learn until he sees it happen. After that he never forgets. This war isn't such a dangerous business if you go about it the right way. I take no chances, so I know I'll come out O.K. I prefer being overcautious. Even though I'm not in the front lines I never go to sleep without having my weapons right next to me. I'd never think of crawling out of my slit trench on a rainy night and going to sleep on level ground to keep dry. I've got too good a life. No, baby, I'll get my Luger all right, but I'll get it the safe way --- by personally winning an argument with some Nazi officer who owns one.

4 CARENTAN

Fate had finally gotten around to my case. I found the Battalion O.P. (Observation Post) at the edge of a hedgerow. It was called an O.P. despite the fact that the only thing you could see was the next hedgerow. The first thing to greet me was the bodies of the German dead. It was difficult to look, but I forced myself anyway. They were sprawled around in various positions, and their faces were all painted black,--camouflage, perhaps. No one else seemed to be bothered by them. American dead, on the other hand, had to be removed promptly, as I discovered afterwards, since no one could stand to look at them. The Germans were left to the Graves Registration people, who would come after the front moved forward.

I did not have to dig in. There were slit trenches to spare, left over no doubt from casualties. That night the shelling was incessant, and punctuated by the screams of the wounded and dying. I could tell that the Medics were going to them, but I lay crouched in my slit trench, afraid to raise my head, never looking up, and feeling completely useless. My initiation into the sight of American dead came when we attacked the next morning. As I moved forward along a hedgerow, he lay right in my path, looking for all intents and purposes as if he were just fast asleep. I stepped over and went on.

The next one was not so easy. I was waiting for the soldier in front of me to fill his canteen from a water bag, so that I could then fill mine, when a high velocity shell came in without warning. There was no time for us to hit the ground. He fell and called out, "Medics." And then he was dead, without a scratch, no doubt due to the concussion. My entire body began to shake violently, and I could not stop shaking for a full 24 hours. No one appeared to take notice,--but then again no one paid much attention to me anyway, or expected me to do anything during those first few days. I also was unable to eat at all for the first three days.

One night I shared a slit trench with another replacement officer. After a particularly bad artillery barrage he said, "You know, a guy could take off for the rear and never be noticed." The next morning he was gone. We heard he had turned himself in, saying he simply could not stand the shelling. The rumor was he was sent back to the States and reclassified to a desk job. I never did hear of any officer being court martialed for desertion.

My first assignment from the battalion commander was to calculate the azimuth of the direction in which we were to attack, from a knowledge of the map coordinates of our position and the objective. But the shelling was so heavy that I simply could not think clearly enough to determine whether to add or subtract the magnetic declination. So finally in desperation I made the choice at random, figuring on a 50% probability of success. The attack seemed to go all right.

When I led the Intelligence Section on my first reconnaissance patrol, as we approached a small footbridge one of the men ran ahead of me saying, "Hold it, Lieutenant, it may be mined. Let me check it first." And before I could think of what to do he had tested it with his own weight. It never blew, and we crossed successfully. Many years later, long after the war was over, the members of the Section who had survived decided to hold a reunion. I was excited at the thought of seeing them again. But too much water had flowed under that bridge. No one seemed to know what to say. We had all gone our separate ways. Men willing to lay down their lives for each other then had become strangers now. The only thing we had in common was the past.

V-Mail   Thur., July 13, 1944

Somewhere in France

Dear Dopey Darling:

I've been too busy to write lately. As you see, I finally have my regular address. I like my outfit --- everybody is swell. I guess war brings out the best in people as well as the worst. I've seen it all now --- I'll tell you about it some day. I'm feeling fine --- haven't got a scratch. The Germans are taking an awful shellacking. They're like cornered rats. They're even pitiful --- begging us not to kill them. Unfortunately they're not the Nazis I've always wanted to get at. They're replacements. There aren't many of the old timers left. These are young boys and elderly men --- Austrians and Poles mixed in with the Germans. Dopey face, there isn't much left to this war. That's why you don't have to worry about me. And I'm really terribly careful --- I take no chances. I definitely intend to pester you for the rest of your life.

I hope we'll be in a rest camp soon, with plenty of time and stationary to write you a nice long letter. Then I'll be able to shave off my nice long beard and take off my shoes, and wash up. All I have with me now is weapons and ammunition. I really travel light --- not like maneuvers. And yet it does resemble maneuvers in some ways --- but not in others.

No time to write more. Give everybody my love --- especially you.

***

Sat'y, July 15, 1944

Some nice safe foxhole in France

Dear Dopey darling:

There's a lull today on the Western front --- at least this particular part of it, so I just shaved off a week's growth of beard and washed my hands and face for the first time since reaching my unit. In case you haven't received the little V-mail letter I wrote the other day, I've been assigned at last. I borrowed this stationary from the Communications Officer, who is a very nice kid. In fact everyone in my new outfit is pretty swell. I guess I'm pretty battle hardened by now --- a week in combat is a long time.

I still feel very ineffectual as far as doing my job is concerned --- but I guess I'll improve. I feel a lot better today, since the same Com O whose stationary I'm using told me he heard the Colonel say that I've caught on faster than any other replacement officer he's ever had. However, I'm still a grave disappointment to myself. I'm far from being the brave hero I hoped to be --- I blush to think of all the times I've wished I were back in Grand Central Palace. War is a terrible racket to be in, baby face. Even a just war is a horrible thing --- not at all the way it is in the manuals at Fort Benning --- and yet it's amazing how the impersonal aspects do follow the training manuals --- the same problems of control and communication. But for the individual there's an immeasurable world of difference. Some day I'll really tell you about it. But I guess I'll forget. Even from one minute to the next you forget. Fear comes in waves. After it's over you begin thinking you're on maneuvers again, and then something happens to remind you you're not. But it's amazing how pliable the human mind is. Even to this you make some sort of adjustment. Life goes on. Right now I'm feeling pretty chipper. You can hear the whine of our own artillery overhead heading for the German lines --- to us this sounds like music --- we call it outgoing mail. You don't feel quite as good when Fritz starts lobbing over the incoming mail. But you can be pretty damn sure there's a lot more outgoing than incoming. It's beautiful to see the air and artillery support they can give us when we jump off in the attack.

Tuesday, July 18, 1944

Still in France, but a little closer to Berlin

Dear Dopey face:

The last letter (above) was interrupted, and a lot has happened since then. I've begun to earn my pay for the first time since I put on a uniform. I've been in so many attacks I've lost count. I've really found a home in this outfit. The Battalion Commander is very pleased with my work, and has spoken so well of me that he's embarrassed me. He's a very good guy --- he always carries out his assignment, but feels the loss of every man personally. Everyone in the battalion is tops as far as I'm concerned --- officers and men. I'm rather pleased with the work I've done myself. I believe I've saved the lives of a number of our boys, and I know I've cost the Germans plenty. Since I've arrived I've encouraged the men to take prisoners, and I've put the screws on them.

> *Prisoners have to be sent to the rear. But when an airborne unit jumps into an isolated area there is no rear. Therefore paratroopers usually don't take prisoners, and as a result when our Division took over from the 101st neither side was taking prisoners. It was a sort of mutual agreement. The custom continued from sheer momentum. I remember coming upon a position a Rifle Company had just taken and asking, "Any prisoners?" and being told, "There was a wounded one right over there, Lieutenant, but I just finished him off."*

The prisoners are very cooperative and tell me everything I want to know --- all I have to do is tell them I'll have them shot immediately if they refuse. The threat never has to be carried out --- I wouldn't anyway, I'm too damn kindhearted. Although I've surprised myself --- I never knew I could be as cold and cruel as I have been on occasion.

Anyway, as soon as we run into some resistance, we get ourselves one or two prisoners, and I find out just how strong the opposition is. Sometimes a small group of men can hold up a large unit for a long time. But I find out that it's only a small group, and instead of screwing around all day, our Battalion pushes right through. On the other hand, when we run into a stronger defensive position, I find out exactly where their lines are, and within two minutes I've got our artillery pounding the hell out of them. The other day, when a couple of our tanks were knocked out, the Germans sent a party up from their Division Engineer Bn. to retrieve these tanks and take them to the rear of the German lines. We captured the Sgt. in charge of the group, and he told me exactly where his Battalion was bivouacked in the rear, and our Artillery straightened them out. I wouldn't be surprised if today the Division no longer has an Engineer Bn. Of course interrogating prisoners isn't my job. I'm a Bn. S-2, but by the time they get back to the IPW team the prisoners have cooled off a bit. But I get them while they're hot. They're shaking with fright and begging me not to kill them, and even after I'm through with them, they're still not sure. I let them know that it would be unfortunate if anything they tell me isn't true. After all, it does no harm to scare them a little --- after they go to the rear they'll have a better life than I have. Anyway, if I can find out exactly where the Germans are, and our Artillery pastes them good, then our battalion walks through with a minimum of casualties.

> *It was not always thus. The first German unit we encountered was the 17th SS Division ("Götz von Berlichingen" on their shoulder patches). The Sergeant I interrogated said he would give me only name, rank, and serial number. So I put the muzzle of a .45 caliber pistol to his stomach and said, "You will answer all my questions!" He simply turned his back, effectively daring me to shoot. But that must have been the last elite unit we encountered, because the prisoners who followed offered little if any resistance to interrogation.*

I had a rather interesting experience the other day. I was making a reconnaissance for a route forward, and I came to a tiny little village. I called out *"Bonjour"* to the civilians, and to my surprise, instead of answering they just turned their backs. It looked like a bad sign, and I had only five men with me. I went through a gate, and asked some Frenchman in my impeccable French, *Ou est le Boche?"*

They all got rather excited, and began whispering, *"Vous Americain? Americain?"* They couldn't believe that the Americans were already there. *"Dangér monsieur. Dangér! Les Boches --ici."* Apparently the Germans were still in town; in fact, two of them were right in that very house. I got scared as hell, and told the Sergeant, "Let's get the hell out of here," which we did, and quickly. But as it turned out the Germans were even more scared than we were, although there were around 30 of them and only 5 of us. We came back in around 20 minutes with the whole Battalion, and then I got the story straight. Apparently we were never expected so soon. The French expected us least of all, and they said that the Germans were wearing field jackets like ours, and the civilians thought we were Germans too. One second they were talking to the Germans, and the next second there I stood. They simply couldn't believe it. It all happened so quietly, without a shot being fired. The French people started dancing around in the streets, and they brought me some cognac to drink, in honor of the fact that I was the first American they had seen since France fell. And that's how this little village was liberated.

Later in the day the Germans had our men pinned down before another little village. The Germans had an SS officer leading them, and you can never get them to surrender when they have an officer. But the Company Commander of our leading company wanted me to take a white flag and go to their lines with a little party, and talk them into giving up, so as to save us some casualties. I didn't like the idea of going forward unarmed that way, especially with a Nazi officer out there. German soldiers are willing to surrender when their officer is dead, but until then they are more scared of him than they are of us. Anyway, full of forebodings, we started out unarmed, with our hands in the air. I yelled, *"Deutsche Soldaten! Wir wollen sprechen."*

> *According to my memory of the event, I walked ahead alone. From my interrogation of prisoners we had taken I was convinced the Germans would not fire at me.*

As we got closer some French civilians stuck their heads out of the windows. Then they came pouring out of the houses, tears streaming down their faces, and wanted to hug us. *"Les Boches --- partis!"* And so it was. The Germans had taken off. When I told the Colonel about it he told me I was never to do anything like that again. And I never will.

I remember he was pretty angry about it. When later the Adjutant wrote up a glowing citation and put me in for a Silver Star, the Colonel knocked it down to a Bronze Star. In a way he was right. Besides the fact that the Germans could have shot me, it was my job to kill the enemy or take them prisoner, not to avoid a fire fight and let them escape. On the other hand, I had taken the objective without suffering any casualties.

Usually if I find out that the enemy has lost its officer I try sending a prisoner back to talk them into giving up. But this business of going over myself, and without a rifle, --- well, the hell with that. I've got a date back in Brooklyn. That's the only time I ever did anything foolish.

In case this is giving you the idea that I'm brave or something, just forget it. Because I'm not. I'm the careful type. I've seen heroism, and I certainly can make no claim to it. The bravest men I've ever seen are the medics. When the air is so hot with lead that the rest of us have our noses buried in the dirt in the nearest crack in the ground we can find, the litter bearers and aid men are moving about completely oblivious to all the danger. They go anywhere the Infantry goes, and because of their work, we have 100% evacuation of wounded, and the number of deaths is kept very low.

I was not about to communicate, nor was I permitted to write, what I must have known by now, namely, that our casualty rate was in fact running well over 100% per month, or that the officer I replaced had been killed on his first day of combat.

Dopey face, I sure would like to write you a nice long letter, but this is being interrupted constantly, and we'll just have to wait. The Germans are on the run, and maybe the whole damn thing will be over by the time you get this. I sure would like to get some mail. Delivery here is excellent; mail comes right up to the front lines all the time, but you don't know my new address, and meanwhile that old mail is still chasing around and I don't hear from you.

I'm feeling in the best of spirits. I'm very happy considering what's going on, and my morale is absolutely tops. How's yours, funny face? I bet I'll see you soon.

***

Thur., July 20, 1944

Somewhere in France

Dear Dopey:

How do you like this fancy stationary I've managed to get hold of? Hold it up against the light and you'll see the Cherbourg seal. Well, baby, it's hard to believe this is me out here. I guess I'm as battle hardened as it's possible for a man like me to become battle hardened. I do my work as well as I can, and nothing surprises me any more. I saw replacements moving up the road the other day, and thought it was very funny the way they fell into a ditch every time a gun went off.

We're still killing Nazis, and driving them back. You'll have to forgive me if my letters are a little on the dull side now. Combat is hardly conducive to letter writing. The mind becomes sluggish. But I'm really doing swell. I like my job, and people depend on me. It makes me feel good to know that I've stood the test. Frankly, as a result of my experiences with my old outfit, I had developed a sort of inferiority complex. That's completely cured now. I'm doing all right.

We got a Nazi Captain today. I think I'll enclose some snapshots he had --- one of himself drinking with his wife --- to the conquest of the world, I guess. He also had some envelopes which will come in handy --- he won't need them, since he's dead.

The news is constantly good. I'm looking for a German crack-up any day now. I wish we could move as fast as the Russians. Don't know how they do it. But we certainly move faster than the Germans. We get them with their pants down.

There's really nothing to write about now. I wrote you some of my "adventures" in the last letter, but somehow it's all mixed up now, and I don't know what happened when, and anyway I'm sleepy. Gee, but I'd like to get some news from home. My goodness, what's happening, anyway?

How is dopey Paulie, and Rivkie, and your parents, and everybody?

As I told you before, everybody in my outfit is pretty swell. I wouldn't want to be in any other one. We have 100% cooperation. I sure miss you something awful though. Please don't worry about me, because nothing can happen to me. I don't know why I'm so sleepy. I've become so adjusted to this racket that I even take time out to brush my teeth every day. It's funny how quiet things get sometimes. At times there may be only 25 yards between us and the Germans, and things are so quiet you wouldn't know there's a war going on. And at other times it sounds like the end of the world.

P.S. How about telling them to send me a ballot, or something? I don't have those nice cards you sent me, and I forgot whom to write. Tell Dewey I want to vote against him, and won't he please send me a ballot. I'm kind of tied up right now, and don't have time to use his fine machinery.

P.S.S. --- I love you too. Yes.

***

Sat'y, July 22, 1944

Somewhere in France

Dear Dopey:

No change in situation. I don't know why it's so hard for me to write these days. After all, here I am in combat, and there should be a lot to write about. But somehow I'm all dried up inside. Things have become a bit quieter recently, and I have a little time to write, but for the first time in my life I haven't the desire. I'm feeling fine, and we're up on the war

60

news, which makes us all very optimistic. We get Stars and Stripes regularly, and somebody's managed to fix up a radio on one of the Communications jeeps, so we know all the swell things that are happening. I'm looking for a quick end to the European war --- even before you get this letter --- but I know it's dangerous to become too confident. You get the urge to ease up --- you figure, better not take any chances, this'll be over soon, and it would be a helluva time for something to happen to you. So you have to watch out for this paralyzing optimism. But it sure is good to feel that the end is in sight. War is hardly my conception of the ideal occupation. I can think of a lot of things I'd rather be doing --- taking a nice walk with you, for instance.

I'm as happy as it's possible to be under the circumstances. My Colonel is a helluva swell guy, the best Battalion Commander I've worked for, and I really feel useful, because he depends on me a lot, and often asks my advice, which makes me feel very good. He's very unaffected, the very opposite of Ondrick --- no airs. If a Company is pinned down and isn't advancing, he clasps his head in his hands and says, "Oh, God, wot'll I do? I just wasn't cut out for this kind of job."

> *On one such occasion a lead Company in the attack was being cut to pieces, and he seemed to freeze up. I took the radio out of his hands and ordered what was left of the Company to pull back for the night. And he accepted it. The attack was resumed the next morning.*

But actually he's very good. And he's got a very lively sense of humor. And of course I like him because he puts so much stock in what I tell him. If I tell him the opposition out in front isn't too strong, he'll order the Companies forward. And since I've been showing him what sad sacks the Germans are, he's been very optimistic.

So you can see things are O.K. with me, dopey. I hope you're equally well. No time for more. Take it easy, pieface. See you soon, I hope.

P.S. --- I got this envelope off my friend the late Nazi Captain I wrote you about. Did you get his snapshots I sent you the other day? The envelope is in pretty good shape considering everything, don't you think so?

5 CUTTING THE *ST.-LÔ-PÉRIERS* HIGHWAY

The Germans would often fight to hold a town in the daytime, and then evacuate under cover of darkness. The only way to find out if they were still there was to send out night patrols. This was my job, and the patrols were made up of men from the Rifle companies, led by a platoon leader. Patrolling an enemy-held town at night was such an unpleasant job that I could not face the men I was sending out unless I had done it myself and they knew it. So the first time I decided to lead the patrol.

It was a moonlit night, and as I entered the town, accompanied by a Sergeant and half a dozen men, the only movement to be seen was of our own shadows. I think I was never so afraid in my whole life. Every doorway, every window, every nook and cranny could bring sudden death. As we passed a barn, suddenly there was the sound of movement inside. We froze, expecting the worst. It was the perfect setup for an ambush. I hesitated for a moment, but there was only one thing to do. "Keep me covered," I said to the Sergeant, and kicked the door open, stepping into the darkness inside.

My finger was on the trigger of the tommy gun, but before I could start firing I was nearly knocked over by the mad scramble of activity caused by what could now be seen to be several pigs rushing out the door, oinking loudly. The Germans had gone, leaving only the farm animals to defend the town. As we made our way back I realized I was completely drenched in perspiration, as if I had been under a shower, even though it was a cool night.

Sat'y, July 29,1944

France

Dear Dopey:

Our forces made such a nice big breakthrough, and the Germans ran so far and so fast that we've found ourselves in what is the next best thing to a rest camp. You've read about it, of course. By now our troops have reached the sea and closed the trap, but yesterday the Germans ran so fast that in our particular sector we closed together and found ourselves well behind the lines. I first realized that I was no longer in the front lines when a field artillery outfit drove past us and we heard the loud hearty laughter of men who are not in contact with the enemy. It was the same contrast I had first noticed when I came up here, only in reverse. You see it in the replacements, as they come marching up the road with brand new uniforms and fancy horseshoe pack rolls (which they'll throw away within two hours), giggling and cracking silly jokes. We were the same way when we arrived, and then it was that I noticed that in the front lines men don't laugh. But that's not really true. It's simply that the humor is of such a quiet and subdued type that to a man arriving from the other world it looks like these men don't know how to laugh. But after you've been along a while you learn the new language, and then you laugh the same way as the others. Then you find yourself in the rear again and hear the loud joking and slapstick ribbing that soldiers always indulged in back in the States. And for the first time you realize that something has happened to you, because you can only smile. Then you start loosening up gradually.

I noticed it when I was in a Replacement Battalion in the rear; --- I went to the hospital and talked with some of the casualties --- how quiet and reserved they were. But it's amazing how quickly people recover. The human organism is pretty well constructed, considering everything.

He's hard to kill, and he heals quickly. Very few of our casualties are KIA's. Most of them are relatively minor wounds. German shrapnel is of a poor quality. There aren't many fragments, and they rely for the most part on the effect of concussion.

> *Where did I ever pick up a story like that, or was I simply lying outright? I was obviously covering up here, since I knew very well from personal observation that approximately 25% of the casualties were KIA's, and that the best I could hope for was to land among the remaining 75%.*

The same is true of their hand grenades. Our stuff slaughters them like cattle, though. The prisoners tell horrible stories of the effect of our bombing and Artillery. The Germans are very good at evacuating their dead. *So were we.* But you still find enough of them.

Our evacuation of the wounded is pretty damn good --- and as a result there are very few deaths for the number of wounded. The wounded are pulled out fast, and handled tenderly. I usually try to carry a needle and some morphine, and if a man is in great pain I give him a shot.

I don't know why I can't find anything else to write about. You know how I am, dopey. I've always written you about what I was doing, and now the subject is a poor one. I wish I could write about something else. If I'd only get some mail I'd be able to. I suppose in another week or so your mail will start reaching me direct, and then it'll be O.K. again. But now I'm hurting. Oh, yes, you can send me a package with some nice things to eat --- also some writing paper. I can get envelopes as much as I want. The Colonel keeps getting packages all the time. Makes me jealous. But I'd rather have a letter than a package any time. In fact, I'd rather have a letter than most anything. The two most important things in combat are mail and ammunition. And we get all the ammo we can use. So that leaves mail.

The civilians in the town we took yesterday told us that the Germans left in great haste, and then bethought themselves, and came back and slaughtered all the cattle. Why, I can't imagine. They must think we rely on the countryside for our food --- which isn't true at all --- or else they're just going crazy with venom and hatred. The French people danced in the streets and threw flowers at our boys.

Enemy prisoners have been of all kinds --- young 17 year old kids and men in their 40's,--Nazi "idealists" (rare) and old soldiers. Most of them are tired and disgusted. We had one Technical Sergeant *(Oberfeldwebel*) yesterday who clicked his heels, stood at attention, and told me everything I wanted to know. He was tired of the war, disgusted with his officers, and apparently quite happy that for him it was all over.

What is there to tell about, pieface? When I see you there'll be enough time. Forgive me if I don't write as often as I used to. Not only is there little time, but it's hard to write, somehow.

We had two Russian prisoners a few days ago. They had been captured on the Russian front two years ago and, like the one I wrote you about before, were used by the Germans to care for their horses.

It's hard to believe today, but the Germans were still relying to some extent on horses to draw their artillery.

We got some interesting documents at a German Battalion C.P. --- among them a Russian diary --- kept right from the day the man was mobilized shortly after Germany invaded the Soviet Union, and kept right up to the very day the document was found. The last entry spoke of the air bombing (you read of the 3,000 plane raid which preceded the big offensive). Then the writer says, "Who knows if anyone will ever read these words? My poor dear children --- will you ever learn what became of your father?" I was feeling all kinds of sympathy till I ploughed through more of the document. I discovered clippings from an anti-Soviet gov't paper printed in Russian, probably by the Germans. There was an item about the "anti-Bolshevist partisans operating behind the Russian lines" --- in the Caucasus, in Red Army units, etc., etc. And in reading more of the diary I discovered that the writer was one of these "partisans," --- only he wasn't operating behind the Russian lines, but behind the German --- which is, I imagine, the usual case. The diary was quite a revelation. I turned it in to the proper authorities.

The stuff the Germans carry is interesting --- much of it is dirty poetry and pornographic photographs. The newspapers are of the Hearst American Weekly type.

Be a good girl, pieface. Write lots of letters and tell me all about yourself. Soon I'll come back to you, I bet. Sweetheart, be good. I love you.

***

American Red Cross stationary: Sunday, July 30, 1944

Ole France

Dear Dopey face:

I am all rested up and wonderfully refreshed. I took a bath, a shave, and a haircut. This is developing into a regular rest camp. I spent the afternoon at a well washing off nearly a month's filth. You don't know how swell it is to be clean again.

And that's about all there is to write --- except that I'm feeling homesick, and should feel not at all disappointed if Germany collapsed tomorrow, or, better yet, yesterday. I feel as though we've licked them already, so what the hell are they still fighting for. But I suppose I shouldn't take that attitude. I've been in less than a month of fighting, so what right have I got to be weary, but after all, there are more pleasant occupations, aren't there?

I wish those SOS stinkers would get some mail to me. It's three months since I said goodbye to you, and in that time I haven't gotten more than around six letters or so from you --- none at all in the last month.

But I suppose you're still there, aren't you? I hope so --- 'cause I'm fixing to look you up right soon --- soon as this here fighting is over.

Anything would be good for a change --- even if it was only that we got out of this damned hedgerow fighting and out on some decent terrain.

But the best change I can think of is the kind of terrain we've got in Prospect Park.

So what's there to write about, funny face? Oh, yes, I forgot to tell you yesterday about the war correspondent who spoke to me in the last battle *(during a lull in the fighting, of course)*, and said that his paper, the New York Sun, would get in touch with you. Did they?

> *They did indeed, the very next day. But the interview was a total fabrication, obviously concocted by an editor back in the States. I was quoted as saying things I never could have said.*

Write me a letter, you little so-and-so. You know, it isn't just war. I'm kind of tired of Army life in general. I've got an awful hankering for civilian life. G'night, dopey.

***

Monday, July 31, 1944

Somewhere in France

Dear *(sister-in-law)* Rivkie:

The Germans tore out of here so fast that we found ourselves well behind our lines, and things have been so quiet in the last couple of days that you'd think we were back in England. We can really use the rest too. So right now I've got a chance to write a little mail. I have your last letter in front of me --- I never had a chance to answer it before --- and reading it again takes me back to the old life I left behind me. I've received no mail since I joined my outfit, which is nearly a month ago. We've been fighting all that time, and a month in the front lines is a long time. It's long enough to leave an impression. Believe me, Rivkie, war is a terrible thing --- even a just war, like this one. It's one thing to fight an impersonal sort of war, where you push buttons or pull strings, like in the Air Corps or Artillery, but this business of living so close to the enemy you can see or hear them, and always looking death in the face, 24 hours a day, is pretty rugged. You walk with a man, talk to him --- he smiles at you, wonders when the war will end --- and then you hear the whine of a shell and drop to the ground --- you look around at him, and he's dead. That's all. Just like that.

I suppose I shouldn't write these things, but a person has to talk to somebody in the other world back home, and I wouldn't say anything like that to Dora or my parents --- and don't you repeat it. You know what I mean --- or at least you have some vague idea. No one can really know in advance. XXXXX don't know, as they come marching up the road with their new uniforms and wise cracks. But they learn quickly.

> *The base censor cut out my words, which must have said "The replacements ..." Was the idea to keep people at home from knowing that there were such things as replacements?*

And then you make some kind of adjustment. A couple of incidents shake you so much that every noise makes you jump for a hole. And after a while your nerves settle and you can look at everything without turning your head. You learn the difference between the way the enemy's machine guns sound and your own, the way a shell whines when it's coming toward you, and when it's passing over. And you find you can smile again, even if you don't laugh --- and you eat and even sleep under fire --- finally you even find time to brush your teeth or shave --- at least every week or so. And life goes on.

I suppose it's really not so bad. There are times when it's quiet and you can relax a little. And there's always the satisfaction that no matter how bad it is for you, it's ten times worse for the Nazis. They're a pretty sad lot, these *Herrenvolk,* when they're losing. There aren't many of the old Nazis left --- just young kids and tired old men. But as long as their officers are alive they're more afraid of them than they are of us. But when they can many of them surrender. One of our officers tells a story with great gusto about how he jumped over a hedge into the midst of about 6 Germans. He grabbed for his pistol, figuring that the jig was up and a burp gun would riddle him in about 1/10 of a second. But the Germans, more quickly than you could bat your eye, clapped their hands over their heads and yelled, *"Kamerad!"* But as long as their leaders are with them they keep their machine guns and mortars firing --- and the amazing thing about the efficiency of German organization is that they can hold an Army together by sheer force. Even the old timers are tired of Hitler and have given the whole thing up as a bad business. But when you ask them why they keep fighting, they just shrug their shoulders and say, "Because we have to." Their officers shoot them for trying to surrender. You can get an idea of the nature of German discipline when I tell you that only about 50% or so are actually Germans. We get Austrians, Poles, Dutch, Russians, everything imaginable. We got two Russians the other day. They had been captured on the Russian front two years ago. The Germans force even them into the Army; the only thing is that they don't arm the Russians --- they use them for menial jobs like caring for horses. But the others are used as fighting soldiers. So you can see what the Army consists of. Even the SS troops consist of green replacements, nothing like the traditional Nazis of old. Now and then you run into the old Nazi arrogance, but it's pretty rare. I guess they've been cut down to size.

Our morale is good, particularly now that the men are getting a little rest. The Regimental Surgeon just came around, and I borrowed a morphine needle off him. I like to carry one with me. Sometimes it takes a little while for a medic to get to a man. And a little morphine can save a lot of pain. I used up my last one.

I keep hoping that the Nazis will give up the ghost any day now --- in fact, maybe by the time you get this letter. Things have never looked as good as far back as I can remember. I even started reading the newspapers. We keep pretty up to date on the news. Our newspaper, "Stars and Stripes," arrives quite regularly, delivery right to the foxhole, as it were.

Talking about foxholes, the most important tool an Infantryman has is his shovel. Hardly a man in my outfit would be alive today if he hadn't dug in every time he stopped moving. The German method in this hedgerow fighting is to hold us up with machine guns at a certain hedgerow, and then lay their mortars and artillery on us, especially mortars. The best thing is to keep moving forwards. The vast majority of casualties are shrapnel, rather than bullet wounds. But when you do stop, you have to dig, and believe me, baby, nobody has to urge you to. It's not like maneuvers. On occasion I've dug in three or four times a day, and with all the interruptions, it's no mean job. There's at least one occupation this war is preparing me for.

I see from your letter that you're all worked up about the favorite American prejudice, race hatred. Well, in the time I've been in the Army I've learned to live with it, and maybe I can give you a few tips, although by now you've probably learned them yourself. First of all, you have to start out by adjusting yourself to the people around you, --- instead of becoming so horrified at the fact that they don't conform to your most basic assumptions, that you alienate them at the outset of the conversation. Don't challenge every wrong statement they make. Wait for the right time, and when they show an opening, ram your idea home. Never get excited, and don't be surprised or shocked at the things they say, because your ideas are probably more shocking to them than theirs are to you. Don't argue every issue. Stick to fundamentals. Put your argument in terms of the ideas and even the prejudices the person already has, and remember that everyone who is a victim of fascist ideology is not necessarily a fascist himself. People are what their society makes them, and race prejudice is a pretty universal trait in our country. Treat it as such, not as a monstrosity or abnormality. All of us are victims, to a greater or lesser degree. Often the ones who talk about it the loudest are the least offenders, and those who say nothing the worst. Don't let this fool you. Frequently people shoot their mouths off in an effort to impress others. If you challenge their opinions violently, they will feel compelled to defend them, but if you talk in a very different way, without actually starting an argument, you'll soon find such people moderating their speech. Then, after a little while you may find an opportunity for a nice talk, which will be a comparison of ideas, rather than an argument. And it's better to talk to one person at a time. Race prejudice is fostered by crowds, just like lynchings. A man will think twice about expressing a point of view when he's alone in his opinion, while his courage is bolstered when he knows that his ideas are those of the mob. When you discover a person who is really hopeless, and an active fanatic, or worse yet, an intelligent Fascist (and don't be too fast about labelling anyone as such), a little wise maneuvering will isolate him --- not by arguing with him, but by talking to the others. But such cases will be rare. Above all, don't give people the impression that you have an axe to grind. Most

Americans are pretty casual about their opinions. They don't like people who make a big issue of what to them is merely "politics" or something.

And above all, don't base your campaign on a person's worst and most deep rooted prejudices. You're only breaking your head against a stone wall. It's a fundamental principle of tactics to commit your greatest strength where the enemy is weakest, instead of where he's strongest. Unfortunately this isn't always done. But if you can make a dent somewheres else you may be able to bypass the worst prejudices, and mop up after you've won him over. As in the case of all formulas, this doesn't always work. But I've found it to be the best way to handle a pretty hard job. You may only start the reconditioning process, and leave it to someone or something else to finish. But it's certainly better than starting a fight. However, I suppose by this time you know all this.

Gee, dopey, won't it be wonderful when this war's really cleaned up? Wow. So long, kid. Be good. See you soon. Love.

***

Monday, July 31, 1944

Somewhere in France

Dear Dopey:

We're still taking life easy. Somebody's radio is on, and I'm listening to a Beethoven concert. It's a wonderful thing for me --- you know how it's always been with me and music. It straightens me out, restores my perspective, brings my mind back to the normal thoughts of peacetime living. I just wrote a letter to Rivky. I've owed her one for some time, but never had the chance. I was feeling a little sour at the beginning of the letter, and I kind of poured out a little of the less pleasant side of my business. Tell her to pay no attention to that part of the letter.

Other replacement officers got some mail today, so I have high hopes of getting something. It sure will mean a lot to me.

I just ate supper, and feel like a million dollars. Please, God, just let me get a letter from you, dopey. I just expressed the idea that that was all I wanted in the world, and our new Executive Officer said that what he'd like most of all is a nasty stinky old ice cream soda (chocolate flavor). I guess next to you I'd like one of those, but after all the two things do go together, don't they? When you're around, an ice cream soda can't be far behind, can it? (Where do I get all those Britishisms in my speech?)

Someone was just telling some yarn about what is supposed to have happened at one of our Corps C.P.'s. A Russian liaison officer who was visiting asked permission to question a German prisoner.

"Do you know what we're going to do to you?" the Russian officer is supposed to have asked the German.

"Yes," said the German. "You're going to shoot me."

"And do you know what is going to happen after that?"

"Yes," he said. "Germany will lose the war."

"And what," the Russian officer is said to have asked, "will happen to Germany after she has lost the war?"

"Germany will no longer exist as a nation," the German said. "She will be cut up into little pieces."

"Yes," the Russian is supposed to have said. "But do you know what will happen then?"

"No."

"Then," the officer said, "the Germans will be cut into little pieces."

---Which amused everybody very much.

Another funny thing that happened was a little talk we got from a General on hedgerow fighting. He brought with him a checkerboard diagram of a set of non-existent theoretical hedgerows, and gave a lecture which his audience of battle-hardened company commanders

73

thought rather amusing. Then way off in the distance a gun went off, and the General jumped as though he was hit, while not a soul in the audience batted an eyelash. I suppose I really shouldn't tell the story. Actually many Generals do go forward. Our Division Executive Officer has spent a great deal of time up in the front lines with us. He is a big man, and struts around with an M1 Rifle slung over his shoulder, booming, "Let's go out there and get those bastards!"

Do I get a letter or don't I. Some replacements who just arrived got some mail. Am I poison or something? And how about some cookies and interesting candy too? Huh, beautiful?

***

Wednesday, Aug. 2, 1944

France

Dear Dopey:

This rest camp stuff slays me. We've gone back to close order drill and calisthenics and inspections. I never thought I'd be doing anything like this over here, but right now I'm at the Regimental C.P., waiting for the General who is our Corps Commander to arrive, so that I can escort him over to our training area. You'd be surprised how full of eyewash our Army is. I've even seen it in the middle of a battle.

We're not supposed to be in a rest camp, but as long as the Germans keep on running we're not needed, and the fellows say it's O.K. with them if they don't stop running till they get to Berlin. Me too.

I'm still convinced that this thing will end in a matter of weeks if not days. I've seen old German Army non-coms who click their heels and stand at attention when you talk to them, but are so sick of the war and disgusted with their officers that they freely give all the information anyone can want out of them. The only thing that holds the Army together is the officer class, and the ones we've run into have been apparently good Nazi fanatics. But they are rapidly dying out. Captured orders reveal cases of 2nd Lts. commanding Battalions, or at most Captains. Usually a Captain or a Major is in command of a Regiment.

Did you hear of this new Combat Infantryman award? Now the Air Corps won't be the only branch to wear special silver insignia, like wings. The doughboy is going to get a great big silver rifle to wear on his chest. Those back in the States who qualify for it by passing certain tests with weapons, etc., will wear the Expert Infantryman's insignia, which is a silver rifle on a blue background. They'll get $5 a month pay increase (big deal), and those who qualify by being recommended for it in combat will wear the Combat Infantryman insignia, which is the same, only with a silver wreath around the rifle, and they get $10 pay increase. This was the "compromise" that came out of Congress as a result of efforts by people to get Infantrymen the same 50% extra pay that the fliers get. There is no harder or more dangerous job than the Private Rifleman has, and people are begrudgingly giving him a little of the credit left over after the glamor boys in the Air Corps have gotten their share. But after all we're not doing this thing for awards or extra pay, are we? Only it does make the guys sore when the Air Corps men get a medal for every five missions automatically, while the Infantryman who attacks every day at a much greater risk gets nothing for it. Ernie Pyle, the doughboy's champion, is doing a lot to get the Infantry some recognition. These things are of course very unimportant. But you know how people are. They like to be appreciated, even if that's not their primary motivation.

Dopey, how soon will it be before I get to see you again? Do you think Japan will put up much of a fight after Germany is licked? I'm inclined to think not, but maybe it's just wishful thinking. War is not my natural vocation. I'm a man of peace. You'd be surprised. You probably think everyone is. But there are a few individuals I've encountered who really take to this killing racket. They're very much in the minority, but they do exist. I find that the thought of you and my parents cramps my style. I can't get you out of my mind, and the result is, when it comes to doing something dangerous I always ask myself if it's really necessary, and if it isn't, I don't do it. I only take the risks that my job requires, and nothing extra. Of course this helps me to survive, but I don't think it makes for very good soldiering. I don't know. Sometimes I wish I had no one back home --- but not for long. It certainly would take a load off my mind. If this were earlier in the war I'd just be fatalistic about the whole thing. But seeing the approach of the end of the war tends to make a man too cautious. Of course it's good to be cautious. But there's a point beyond which it isn't good. Anyway, I try to do my duty. If everybody did that I guess things would go all right. Not everybody has to be a medal hunter. I certainly am not.

About the bravest man I've seen is my Battalion Commander. He's not only brave but very lucky. I guess a man doesn't have time to be brave long if he isn't lucky. But the Colonel is really a swell guy. There isn't a thing I wouldn't do for him. Although he is a West Pointer, he's very unaffected (I think he's only 29 years old), and has a simple type of native intelligence which I think is remarkable considering his background. And a sense of humor --- which is a big thing, I think. And he has a fundamental sense of duty which is very strong --- a hatred for the Nazis and strong feeling for all his men --- he's certainly not the careerist that Ondrick was. He's a tall lanky Texan, and wins everybody over, including his superiors.

Well, I'm beginning to wonder if the General will ever come. As the Colonel said, won't it be just too bad if he doesn't. These high ranking officers always feel that some criticism is required from them, and they will usually pick something ridiculous to make an issue of, instead of sticking to fundamentals. But I saw the Corps Commander yesterday, and he doesn't seem to be a bad sort.

Still no mail from you. I get madder every day. Most of the other replacements are in the same boat. It'll come soon though, I know. You must have my new address by now. But I'm afraid all the mail written to my old APO is hopelessly lost. So you'd better give me a summary of everything that's happened to you since I left, or I won't know what you're talking about. It'll be like starting a book in the middle. I'll never forget that V-mail letter I got from you, labelled page 2 (cont.), and how I sweated trying to figure out what it was all about. So you'd better write me a summary. What happened to your school work, how did you make out in your exams, Calculus, etc.? Did you go on vacation, do you still love me, etc., etc.

I just felt the top of my head, and there's a round bump from wearing my helmet so long. I hope you don't mind. I guess when I'm demobilized it'll take quite a while to get used to going around without a helmet.

By God, if I don't get a letter soon, I'll be very very angry. And <u>send me a package too, with a lot of eating stuff.</u>

And how are all the other people? Little Paulie and your parents and grandma and my parents? Oh, Jesus, send me a letter, baby.

***

Sat'y, Aug. 5, 1944

Dear Dopey:

The kind of war I've been fighting lately is great fun. You just march from town to town --- with the enemy in headlong retreat out ahead of you --- outside of a few snipers and scared Polish boys in German uniform there's nothing to stop you from liberating one city after another. The French people line the streets jumping up and down yelling, *"Vive l' Amerique!"* and insisting on shaking hands with every soldier. Every housewife stands there with a jug of cider, or maybe a bottle of cognac (not so common), or maybe even wine (rare), and a little glass and keeps filling the glass and offering it to every soldier as he goes past. The boys are pretty good about it too. When the order comes down that there will be no more drinking they stop at once. And a good thing, because if they drank everything the French beg them to, they'd be stewed in no time. When you refuse to drink, the people become very unhappy, and plead, *"Pour la France, monsieur! Kaput le Boche!"* They can't understand why, once their own particular town has been liberated, we don't all stop and have one big celebration. Every man, woman, and child has to shake hands with every soldier, and the old women stand in the middle of the street clapping. An old man comes out with a big drum, and starts beating out a martial air, as he marches up and down the block, looking very serious and ceremonial. There's nothing the people won't give *"les Americains."*

As long as the Germans are in headlong retreat they can't even shell us. The only casualty we had yesterday in the Battalion was one man who was hit in the arm by a "sniper's" bullet. A lot of this stuff about snipers is nonsense. Some French people said they were receiving fire from the woods yesterday, and I went out hunting for snipers, but all I could find was some American G.I.'s who were shooting their guns into every tree where they thought they could see some movement.

It looks like the horrors of war are behind us now --- all that seems to be left is a march of liberation. The prisoners tell me that practically the whole German Army is demoralized, --- the only thing that still manages to hold them together by a few thin strands is terror --- they're still afraid of their officers. And they're also afraid of us, because they've been told that we shoot prisoners, and many of them believe it. They run away from their officers and hide in a farmhouse. The French people run after them with knives, the Americans flush them out with tommy guns and hand grenades, and their own officers shoot them. So they don't know where to turn. A Polish 17-yr. old boy told me yesterday that the French people tried to cut him up because they thought he was German. But the French recognize the Russians apparently. Yesterday we got three jolly Cossacks. They had been captured by the Germans near Kharkov three months ago. The Germans put them in German uniform and put them to work. They escaped several times in the Cherbourg fighting and ended up in German hands again. Over here they ran away from the Germans, were taken in and hidden by the French, who gave them civilian clothes and fed them. Then when we entered the city they came over to us. They were so delighted to find an American who spoke Russian that they jumped up and down and talked a blue streak. I piled them in my jeep and took them to the rear. Their homes were in Turkestan and they looked very Oriental. They had been taken through Odessa when it was still in German hands. They said that originally the Germans tried to form a Battalion of Russian troops, but in the first battle they went over to the other side, so since then the Germans have given it up as a bad business, and have been using the Russians only for work. But a couple of nights ago we got a Yugoslav. One of our patrols picked him up at night heading for our lines without a weapon, in order to give himself up. He gave us a lot of information.

Yesterday I got curious about the Germans' psychology, so I asked one of them what he thought of the Nazis.

"What Nazis?" he said. "The Nazis are all back in Berlin working in offices."

"What do you think of Hitler?" I asked him.

"Hitler is a great idealist," he said. "But he's impractical --- his ideals could never succeed."

"Since when is murder an ideal?" I asked, but it isn't my job to convert Germans, is it? It surprised me, though, to learn that even though these people are fed up with the war and the Nazis, they have no hatred for Hitler. He's sold himself to such an extent that they can't believe him capable of anything but the noblest of feelings. But they know the jig is up. They tell me that practically everyone knows it, but they don't know what to do about it. They can't decide whether to surrender or not. They're still afraid we may shoot them.

But I can't get over my three Cossacks. I told them the latest war news, and when I added that pretty soon it looked like they'd be going home, they got so excited I thought they wanted to eat me up. They were about the happiest men I'd ever seen.

And so we march through France, bombarded more with flowers now than by bullets. As we move up a road, the machine guns mounted on our jeeps are covered with garlands of roses.

The further we penetrate the more Russians we find. I just this minute got a report that a lot of Russians have been picked up around here. They carried marks of torture, slits across their bellies, and had fingers lopped off. They explained that every time they refused to obey an order the Germans would cut off a finger. It's hard to believe that these scared German boys that we take are capable of atrocities, but I guess they just sing a very different tune when we get them. I'll tell you one thing --- I've never hurt a prisoner, but I take it out on them by nearly scaring them to death. One kid yesterday was so scared he couldn't talk.

He just stammered and shook like a leaf. It's amazing how strong the desire to live can be.

Still no mail from you, funny face. But the end of the war seems so close that I keep having visions of running up the stairs to your house, and that somehow makes up for it partly.

Meanwhile I'm as happy as can be expected. My Bn. C.O. is tops as far as I'm concerned. I like the men in my outfit. I've got a good Sergeant *(he would die soon in Luxembourg)* and a swell bunch of boys. We took pictures today crowded around and on my jeep. I don't know how long it will take to ever get them developed though.

But wow, do I need some mail. I can't wait for it to start arriving direct to this address. It's a whole month since I got even those two little V-mail letters.

That's enough writing for you, you lazy little good-for-nothing. I bet you're not even writing me --- probably found yourself one of those there aviators who get to go home after flying a certain number of missions. I'll slaughter you when I get home if it's so. So long, baby.

6 *ST.- MALO*

The war had not ended. We had been moved in 2 1/2 ton trucks to Brittany, where we were attacking now in a westerly direction, with orders to take the port of St. Malo. After having undergone decompression and reentered the world of the living, I now had to reverse the whole process. Again it became necessary to accept the idea of death, knowing that every day, 24 hours a day, any minute could turn out to be the last. The adjustment was not as hard as the first time, but by no means easy. And there was no point in burdening the people back home with this problem.

Thur., Aug. 10, 1944

Dear Dopey darling:

I've been getting all your mail fine now. It takes about 10 days to get to me. The old mail is apparently lost. It's really wonderful to get mail nearly every day. I haven't gotten any packages or your cable either, so you see it's silly to send cables, since letters arrive sooner. The V-mail doesn't fare any better than the air mail, I believe. Packages take a long time.

I haven't had time to write for several days, because we have been pretty busy again. These past few days I've seen some very interesting things. I personally negotiated the surrender of a German fortress which held us up for several days in our attack on an important city. The fortress was the key to the defenses of the city and was an immense rocky structure which offered observation and dominated the terrain for miles around.

I believe this fortress was called St. Joseph. The fortresses had been designed to defend against an invasion from the sea. But now they had to turn their guns the other way, because we were attacking from the other direction.

The war has become much more interesting now that the hedgerow fighting is behind us. The terrain is a bit more along the classic style of Benning School for Boys, and you could actually see what was happening for a change. We blasted hell out of the fort with artillery and mortars for a couple of days and finally reached a point where we could see them running around the top crazy with fear, trying to escape our murderous fire.

We were using big 4.2 inch chemical mortars, but firing high explosive rounds instead of the chemical weapons they were designed for.

They looked like clay pigeons in a shooting gallery. I couldn't resist the temptation to grab a B.A.R. and shoot them down like ducks. It was a real field day for us. Just when we were about to assault the place they stuck out a white flag and a party led by a Lieutenant came out to talk to us. They said they wanted to negotiate a surrender. I went back into the fort with them to talk with the garrison commander, a very haughty Nazi Major. What I saw when I got inside was like something out of this world --- subterranean passageways with electric lighting, railroad tracks running through the fort, smashed weapons and equipment all over, self-propelled 150 mm. howitzers. --- And hundreds of Germans standing around watching me as I stalked through the place, with a tommy gun slung over my shoulder. I was the only man in the place who was armed. The Germans had destroyed all their weapons. It gives you a funny feeling to realize that one minute you are killing people as if they were insects, and the next minute you are talking to them as if they were human beings. The Major wanted my Colonel to come in and talk to him personally. Nothing doing, I said. If he wanted to talk to my commander he would have to go outside. How about meeting half way, they asked. Nope, I said. All the way or nothing. So back we walked out of the fort again, I marching along with the German Major and Lieutenant.

(Lt.-)Col. Norris saluted the Major, who returned with the Heil Hitler salute. Then the German Major very pompously and ceremoniously proceeded to proclaim his surrender. "As commander of the fortress of ---- I am forced, because of lack of ammunition and water, because of excessive casualties, and because there is no way to care for the wounded, to surrender the fortress of ----." He was trying to be very dignified about the whole thing, and I kept cramping his style, because the Colonel lost interest and told me to go ahead and make all the arrangements. Inside I found a Russian Lt. Col. and another Russian officer, as well as a few enlisted men. They were wearing the German uniform with the *ROA* insignia *in Cyrillic letters* (Russian Volunteer Army, or some such nonsense).

"What are the Russians doing here?" I asked the Major.

"They are the Russian Volunteer Army," he said. The expression he used was *"freiwillige."*

"Freiwillige?" I asked.

"Ja."

I started talking to the Russians, who told me the usual story, how they were captured on the Russian front, and forced into the German Army at the point of a gun.

"Freiwillige!" I said to the Major very sarcastically. This really burnt him up, especially when he heard me talking Russian.

"Your German isn't good enough!" he snapped at me. "From now on we will use an interpreter!"

"O.K." I said.

The interpreter turned out to speak such bad English that we had to go back to talking German again.

83

Meanwhile I continued questioning the Russians. The German Major told them quietly to keep their mouths shut. I overheard him. *"Ich stelle hier die Fragen!"* I told him. "I'm in command here."

I promised that we would take care of the German wounded, of which there were a couple hundred, and he guaranteed that there were no mines or booby traps. He went around grumbling to his officer, "Oh if I only had three hand grenades, I'd never have surrendered!" The place was full of potato mashers and mortar shells, so that was an awful lie. However, I didn't argue the point with him.

The Russian Lt. Col. was a very friendly guy, with the typical Russian smile. He told me the whole story later. One or two of the Russian soldiers had asked me if we would have them shot. I was becoming curious about this. Nearly every Russian we've ever taken has asked me if I would have him shot, in spite of the fact that I spoke to them in such an obviously friendlier tone of voice than I used with German prisoners, whom I like to keep guessing about their fate. And yet after the conversation was over, the Russian would invariably say, his face creased with smiles, "Then you won't shoot me?" And I would say, *"Nu, konyechno nyet!" "Of course not."* Well, I've solved the problem. The Germans had a Russian Battalion commanded by this Lt. Col. In the very first battle they surrendered to our troops (not my Battalion, but another unit) without firing a shot. Only a few didn't get away, and they were here in the fort. In order to counteract this the Germans have been spreading reports that all Russians found by us in German uniform are shot. The Russians don't know whether to believe it or not, since there is a certain distorted logic in this. So that explains why they feel like hugging me when they discover that I speak Russian and can reassure them.

Fri., Aug. 11, 1944

I am mailing home my Purple Heart. It was quite cheaply won, but at least Carl isn't ahead of me on that over there in the Pacific. I got a couple of tiny splinters of shrapnel in my leg, but I didn't even have to be evacuated. The medics just picked them out. I didn't intend to have it treated at all, but it looked like it was becoming infected, so I had them clean it up. It's all healed now.

Dopey darling, your letters are all arriving. Just got another one last night. Please don't worry about me, silly. It's not as bad as you might think. Look what a racket I've got. I get a Purple Heart for just a scratch like that. Please don't let my work upset you and your school work and all. I'll be O.K. You really overestimate me. I take no chances. Only an accident would really harm me, and accidents take place in civilian life too.

My letter to you was interrupted yesterday, because there was a big gun firing on us, and I had to go up and locate its position and help adjust our Artillery fire on it. We shot hell out of it. This Artillery stuff is a lot of fun. We captured some excellent German telescopes back at the fort, and they helped me find the gun. I could actually see the flash every time it fired. It gives you real satisfaction when you personally are bringing a whole Artillery Battalion down on a Nazi position. I've got an awful lot to write you. But no time now. Be good, baby face. I love you too. But you overestimate me by far. However, that's love, I guess.

7 DINARD

My jeep usually followed in the rear when we were in combat and would only try to reach my position at night when the situation and terrain permitted. But it played an important role when we were chasing the enemy along a highway. The Battalion would ride in two and a half ton trucks, and the idea was to move as fast as possible and still not have the trucks run into an ambush. I was the point in this motorized movement, and rode a half mile or mile ahead of the caravan, with the windshield down flat and an air-cooled machine gun mounted on the hood. A second jeep --- the getaway vehicle --- followed at a distance where it could keep me in sight without itself being caught in the ambush. My driver and I were of course expendable. I would have to provide covering fire with the machine gun, while he would try to bring the vehicle back around. But as it turned out I never had to fire that gun "in anger." The French civilians always saved us by telling me where to find the Boches, and I did not hesitate to stop and ask. Radio contact with the Battalion made it possible for them to keep a safe proper distance. When I located the enemy position I would radio back the information, the troops would detruck, and there was plenty of time to take up battle positions for the attack.

Friday, Aug. 11, 1944

France

Dear Dopey:

I just took a bath and once more I am a nice clean boy. We came up to our present position through a route which took us quite a ways to the rear, and we saw many cute girls on bicycles and civilians and everything, just like in peace time. We are all in the best of spirits as a result. In general, the old timers (I am considered an old timer by now) have made such an adjustment to this kind of life that when not actually under fire they act quite normal. The old tenseness and strain is gone. We can relax and kid around just like anybody else.

Back in the last area we captured a German hospital with medical officers, nurses, patients, and all. I mosied over to see what information I could pick up. The approach was quite different from the one I use during the heat of combat. I just oozed the officer and gentleman, and we all became very friendly. As a result I picked up some interesting items, besides getting a good insight on some of these people. I became particularly chummy with a 1st Lt. who was a Company Commander in a unit which counter-attacked us (unsuccessfully). He was a patient in the hospital --- busted arm. He asked me if he mightn't go to a house in another part of the city and gather up all his belongings, and I put a guard on him and let him go. The German officers are always very concerned about being allowed to take their baggage with them when captured, --- quite a difference from us --- we just wear coveralls and carry nothing but our weapons, a canteen of water, and a spoon. Anyway, we became very chummy during the course of the day, and had some nice interesting talks. I also spoke to one of the nurses and a couple of medical officers and some of the enlisted men. They all claimed that Germany would win the war yet. I don't think most of them believed it. But they didn't trust each other, and were afraid to say anything. They sing a different tune when you get them alone. I asked one of the medical officers whether he was a Nazi. "That's a personal question," he replied. I've never yet found a German who would admit to being a Nazi.

ADOLPH BAKER

"You really believe Germany can still win?" I asked the nurse.

"Natürlich!" she said, with a big broad smile. She was a typical blonde German girl, very pleasant and friendly. I think she was the only one in the whole crowd who believed it.

I started a discussion with the *Oberleutnant* on the possibilities of surrender of the last remaining fortress --- the one which had as its mission to deny us the use of the harbor. "The order has been given to defend to the last man," he told me.

"But why?" I persisted. "So many men will have to die for nothing. You know we'll take it eventually."

"We've got lots of food and ammunition," he said. "And it's protected by a heavy wall of solid rock."

"The fortress of ---- was protected by solid rock too," I said. "And they surrendered."

"They had no ammunition left," he said.

"That's their story," I told him. "I was there, and there was plenty of ammunition."

He shrugged his shoulders. "This one won't surrender. Its construction is much better."

"But what does the whole thing accomplish?" I asked him.

He looked at his broken arm, and the bloody bandages. "What does the whole damn war accomplish?" he asked me. "What difference does it make who wins the war? Men will lose anyway --- the white men. The yellow race is the one that will come out on top." --- Which just goes to show the underlying cynicism and doubt beneath the big front they put up, and the contradictions between the Nazi race theories and their political alliances, which are not lost upon the people.

The medical men asked me later whether we fire at their Red Cross or not, and I told them we don't. They said they don't fire at ours either.

88

We both disagreed slightly on the consistency of this, but finally were willing to agree that there might have been accidents, mistakes, or other exceptions.

"Maybe it's true," I said, "that Germany observes the provisions of the Geneva convention in fighting the Americans and British, but how about the Russians?"

"Well," they said, "the Russians don't observe them either."

"What can you expect," I said, "when your men murder their civilians --- women and children?"

"Well," they countered, quite logically, "they all fight us. There are no non-combatants in Russia. How can we treat them as civilians?"

Oh, hell, I'm tired of writing about the enemy. It's all so screwy. One minute you're killing them, and the next you're holding philosophical discussions.

You're very silly, to make such a fuss over me. Everybody out here is in the same boat. There's nothing wonderful about it. I'm sorry that "Sun" story didn't please you. I didn't think it would be so hot. The correspondent didn't appear to be too clever. And I don't for the life of me know what message he said I was sending you. All I wanted was for him to let you know that he had seen me and that I was all right. I didn't send any message. I can send my messages through the mail. Anyway, I'm curious to know just what they did print. I guess I'll get your letter with the clipping in a day or two. I think it's a good idea your sending both a V-mail and air mail letter every day. Some days I get one and some days the other.

Yesterday I got your V-mail telling about how you want to be as good a horseman as I am, and are going to a dude ranch, which is a very good idea, incidentally. But what was funny about it was that I had just been riding a German horse --- a beautiful one --- the Germans really have nice horses. I wanted to keep him, but I guess it wasn't practical. I'd have to keep him tied to my jeep, and how could I feed him? We're using so much German equipment that pretty soon we won't be able to tell ourselves apart. We eat German potatoes, and German eggs, and German marmalade. If the old German saying has any truth to it, --- *"Man ist was er isst"* --- we really will be Germans soon.[1] The men are wearing German boots, and carrying German pistols and field glasses, and I've got a German BC scope, which we were using to adjust Artillery fire yesterday.

You're so smart, getting a 100% on your Math reexam. You're a little old genius. What are you taking in school during the summer, and what will you take this fall?

I don't have time right now to read all your letters again and answer them, but you're a dopey kid anyway. But very nice nevertheless. Have a nice vacation, darling dopey.

***

Tuesday, Aug. 15, 1944

France

Dear Dopey darlin':

Don't worry about the letters you've got sailing around the globe. I got around 20 of them yesterday. And I'll get the rest. I got two letters today dated Aug. 3 & 4. No, I never got your cable. Probably get it in a month or two.

Hey, dopey, I'm sending you a nice war trophy --- a German Leica camera. It was a present from a Nazi officer --- from him to me to you. I'm sure he had no objection to your getting it --- at least, he never said a mumblin' word. *He came out of a pill box with his hands up and the camera strap around his neck.* It's loaded, and takes 40 pictures, so before I send it I'll take the pictures. Only I don't know how to develop them. The Base Censor now accepts only developed films for mailing, and they say you've got to have them developed through your PX. --- It gets me how all these regulations are made up for the button boys in the

---

[1] Editor's Note: The phrase "Man ist was man isst" can be translated into "you are what you eat".

90

SOS who sit on their asses back in the rear. Where will combat soldiers ever find a PX? But I'll take the pictures and try to get them developed through our Division Signal Company --- and then I'll mail them to you. It's a nice little camera, with a range finder. You just bring the two images together, and it automatically focuses the lens. I'm trying to figure out all the gadgets on it.

We've finished cleaning up another big city. The same old thing happened. We fight for the city, and as soon as it's cleaned out some other outfit moves in to garrison it while we get shipped to another sector. It happens every time. As soon as we get settled in some beautiful hotel or chateau, orders come in to move at once. Anyway, we're getting a breathing spell of a couple of days. This last time the fighting went pretty easy --- we suffered practically no casualties at all. In one day alone our Battalion must have taken nearly a thousand prisoners. If you figure that a Battalion has from six to eight hundred men, you can see how the fight is going. One bunker held out after everything else had fallen. When we finally got it I asked the Major who commanded it why he held out so long.

"Es war ein Befehl," he said.

"To the last shell?" I asked.

"To the last shell," he replied.

"Well," I said. "Was it the last?"

"Ach," he said. "Maybe there were still a few left."

We got nine officers out of that deal, and I packed them all into one jeep, together with their baggage, duffel bags and all. They looked funny as hell --- arms and legs sticking out of the jeep in all directions --- these haughty *Herrenvolk* --- while their men looked on with hatred, and the French civilians hurled insulting remarks after them. The French have a field day every time we capture some high Nazi officers, who just a few hours previously were terrorizing them. The day of retribution has come for the Quislings too. The French want to tear them to pieces --- especially the women who slept with the Germans. They get captured with their supermen right in the pill boxes and bunkers, and the civilians try to kick them and beat them as we march them back. I turned two of these women over to the French gendarmes who are already strutting around in their snappy uniforms. The civilians said they only wanted to shave off these women's hair to humiliate them, and that they would then turn them loose. But some French women who were "nurses" in a German hospital appealed to us for protection against the Resistance, or guerillas, who had threatened to kill them all when night came. And so destiny is finally catching up with these world conquerors and their consorts. The members of the Resistance are a rugged bunch of boys. They are completely armed with German equipment and weapons.

Not that they differ in this respect from our G.I.'s so much. I've gotten an extra jeep and a German truck, but I'm afraid I won't be able to keep these things. Yesterday we reached the point where our Battalion was entirely motorized with German vehicles, but we have to turn that stuff in, damn it. The button boys in the SOS get it. Anyway, I got me a Leica. Normally I don't do any looting of prisoners or the dead, but a camera is military equipment, and a lawful trophy. If I hadn't taken it someone else in the rear would. I did some more riding yesterday. But these horses weren't as good as the ones of the day before. They were Artillery horses, and weren't bridle wise.

The communications section is now using a German switchboard, and we also have one or two German telephone sets. All this equipment is better than ours in many ways, but in any event it means that we have that much more equipment.

I've been fooling around with the camera, but have decided to give it up as a bad business. Even one of my boys who is a camera addict couldn't figure it out entirely because of all the gadgets on it. So I'll just send it home to you. They tell me there's a place in New York called Willoughby's that has instruction booklets and all that kind of stuff, so you can dope it out.

It's raining outside today (oh, yes, I'm in a house). First rain in weeks. Oh, you needn't feel so sorry for me. I live quite well. It isn't like maneuvers. We use houses a lot. These French houses are well built.

(Jesus Christ, the last time I said that I won a Purple Heart. "I bet this house can take a direct hit," I said, and the words were no sooner out of my mouth than --- ka-whoom! --- and the whole room turned black and the dirt was so thick you could scoop it out of the air with your hand, and my leg was stiff and shaking and wet with blood. But it turned out to be just a scratch.) Anyway, we live quite well. There's certainly plenty to drink --- wine, cider, whiskey, cognac, everything imaginable. And I'm never as bored and miserable as I used to be on maneuvers. And you meet so many different people and see so many things. Think of how easily a man can write a book who has been through all this.

Anyway, what a shame it's raining today, just when we've gotten the big news about the invasion of the Southern coast of France. It's funny how it rained at the beginning of our invasion too, and then the weather became beautiful. And now the same thing is happening.

I took a bath today --- the second one in only two or three days. I found time for a bath just before the last battle, and manage to keep quite clean generally. This house we're in now actually has running water, only you have to pump it up downstairs.

Don't worry about me, sweetheart. It won't be long now, and the fighting gets easier and easier as time goes on. The Germans are becoming very demoralized. It's coming to an end now.

Please enjoy your vacation, will you? And get a nice tan --- to impress me when I get back. I was thinking about you when we got news of the Southern landing. You were still sleeping, lazy. (There's a great big German police dog standing here looking at me, with his tongue hanging out. You think he's a spy?)

I'm feeling swell --- get mail every day --- I'm in a swell outfit --- winning the war --- be home soon --- got a cute dopey wife --- getting a lot of traveling done. What's there to complain about?

Well, they promised us (the Corps Commander himself) that after we completed this last operation we'd go to a rest camp. --- The outfit has never been pulled back to a rest camp yet --- they keep using us again and again. But now I don't care any more. General Eisenhower says we've got to get in the knockdown blow, and I guess he's right. Better to keep on socking these guys without giving them a chance to reorganize. This way the war will end that much sooner. Anyway, I'm not tired --- I was yesterday --- I could hardly stand up, and my mind was so foggy from lack of sleep that I was only partly conscious; but I slept late this morning, and I'm all set again.

Don't worry about your old job. Who cares whether they fire you or not? Do your work and pay no attention to them. Anyway, they won't fire you. Have a nice vacation, sweetheart. So long, baby.

***

Around Wed., Aug. 16, 1944

Same ole France

Dear Dopey:

No mail from you today. Wot a gyp. But I got a stack of letters yesterday --- old mail. I think that about brings me up to date, or nearly so, on those lost letters that I thought I'd never see again. I feel as if I'm really in communication with you again. You're so silly to make such a fuss about me in your letters. Just because a guy writes big time doesn't mean he is. When the shells start sailing around, literary skill is of little value. And I'm too careful to have done anything outstanding. I really should take more chances than I do.

Life is soft again. We've reached the sea, and there's no place further we can go, so we're just sitting around again. It's really a wonderful feeling to walk and ride around without anybody shooting at you. Really a luxury. But it's beginning to become monotonous. Before long the brass hats start coming around to inspect our training and heckle us generally. One good thing about the front lines is that there's so little brass around. Lt. Col. is the highest rank I like to deal with. When you get above that they don't know what being shot at is like. I don't see why they don't leave these boys alone and let them sleep and lie around and relax. But no. Down come all the fancy training schedules made up by the swivel chair strategists. Close order drill, calisthenics, etc., etc. If we ever get to a rest camp I'll probably go crazy with boredom. If we could get to a town and have a little fun, or if we could just do what we please it would be all right. If I get back to the States and have to go on maneuvers again, or something like that, I don't know how I'll stomach it.

I've been taking pictures with my new Leica of some of the German pill boxes. I don't know how to use the damn camera, but I may as well use up the film before sending it home. I also had some pictures taken of me, but I don't know how I can develop them or if they'll come out.

I understand that I can discuss operations that are two weeks old or more. When I joined my outfit it was moving South from Carentan, and eventually we took part in the drive which cut the St. Lo-Perier highway. It was right near this highway that I met the Sun correspondent (I still haven't gotten the clipping, by the way). He and the other correspondent wanted to know if it was safe to drive down the highway. But there were still occasional stray bullets whizzing down the road, so we sent them around another way. It was across that highway that I made a reconnaissance for a line of departure in our attack, and I found the line of departure in German hands, and myself in a village still occupied by the Germans. After we had crossed this highway and attacked down it a way, our armored columns went slashing through the German lines in a wide sweep which made the German position untenable. We all closed the big pincer behind the armored columns and found ourselves way behind our lines. That was when we got several days rest. Soon everybody began to find out where everybody else was again. (After a major breakthrough the situation finally becomes nearly as chaotic for the attacker as for the retreating enemy. That's when you just have to stop and reorganize.) Then we swung west to mop up.

The armored columns leave tremendous bypassed pockets of resistance for the Infantry to clean up. After some more time has elapsed I'll tell you what cities we took subsequently, and the name of the fortress whose surrender I negotiated. Incidentally, in the drive on the St. Lô-Périers highway we got the biggest aerial preparation I've ever seen in my life. Since we were in the front lines, the bombs dropped only a short distance from us, and the concussion was so terrific that it was like a huge earthquake. The ground shook, houses crumbled, windows shattered, and we all prayed that the Air Corps wouldn't make any mistakes, however small. You remember reading of the big bombardment in which 3,000 planes took part? Well, that was it. These things are very risky for front line troops, and require the most exact air-ground liaison to avoid accidents. Actually there's always some error, but the help these preparations give us in softening up the enemy far exceeds the harm they do in inflicting a number of casualties on our own troops. It's the same with Artillery. Still, it's a terrible feeling when your own Artillery starts falling short on your position.

Anyway, here I am now, without the least indication that there's a war going on. We had steak and french fried potatoes for supper this evening. Everything we had was German except the steak itself. It's getting so that we won't need any American supplies again. All you can see is German knives, pistols, field glasses, belts, horses, cars, motorcycles, bicycles. We eat German eggs, potatoes, coffee, tea, butter, and the men are even starting to wear German boots and jackets.

The news from Southern France indicates that the Germans are abandoning the defense of France apparently.

And don't get so excited over me. Any City College boy could wax as interesting about all the things I've been through. No kidding. I should be doing a lot of unusual things, and should be a lot braver than the others. But I'm just working along, not sticking my nose or rear end up any higher than necessary --- never hesitating when I have a job to do --- but still not doing anything beyond the call of duty. So I don't know. I'm a little dissatisfied with myself. You and my parents never leave my mind --- still, the others have families too, and I've seen individuals who don't seem to give a damn at all about their personal safety --- and I don't believe the war means as much to them as it does to me. They're generally the ones who get the medals. Of course there are others, like Col. Norris, who has a tremendous sense of duty (and he's a West Pointer). He was hit in the leg by a bullet the same day I was hit, and he refused to leave his post in spite of the pain and discomfort. Now people like that make me feel very modest. And your attempts to make a hero out of me seem silly. It makes me very ashamed when I think that I seriously considered allowing myself to be evacuated that day, when the Colonel, with a much more serious wound, wouldn't even think of it. He lost his S-3 that day too, when he got a bullet stuck in his arm, and I was badly needed, and yet if I hadn't been ashamed I'd probably have gotten myself evacuated. The S-3, incidentally, turned up again around a week later, with his arm in a sling. I think he just ran away from the hospital --- said he couldn't stand it, he was so bored. And I've always considered this S-3 an awful jackass. You just can't judge people entirely by the way they talk or write. The S-3 usually talks and acts in such a stupid way that he's rather unpopular with everyone except the Colonel. But in a fire fight he goes running out ahead of everybody else, and often turns around to find the rest of the Battalion way behind him. What is it --- bravery or foolishness? Who knows? I've seen many brave men --- and I've seen some pretty bad cowards too.

Hey! Somebody just offered me a hundred bucks for the Leica camera, but I wouldn't take it. That camera is yours. So long, baby face.

***

Friday, Aug. 18, 1944

France

Dear Dopey:

We are having a fine time doing nothing, only I think we all have fleas. If it's not fleas it's something else, but I know it's something. I went swimming yesterday in a beautiful stone quarry. I took some pin-up pictures like Carl sent Sherry, but I don't know if you'll ever get the pictures, or if they even come out. As you know, there is no provision for having pictures developed if you're in combat. I took a lot of pictures --- some of them of historical value. I have one of a certain fortified island being bombed *(Cezembre, if my memory is correct)*, and another of a great fortress (whose name I can't tell you yet) shortly after it surrendered yesterday, with the Stars and Stripes flying over it. Some of the pin-up pictures are pretty bad, but I had to outdo Carl. I am sending you the camera today. I have it all wrapped up and ready to go. Somebody offered me $225 for it, and I'm scared to keep it any longer. It's a little bitty thing, but I made a big package out of it (the mail orderly just now came in and picked it up). I also put in the package my Combat Infantryman badge, which came through yesterday. You can keep it for me till I come home, or wear it if you want to. It's a pretty pin --- a silver rifle on a blue background with a silver wreath around it. All the combat soldiers and officers in my Regiment got one --- "for meritorious service in action against the enemy," or something like that, the order reads. The men get a $10 pay increase, but we still haven't got it straight whether the officers do or not. This is supposed to be a sop thrown the doughboy in lieu of the 50% extra pay the Air Corps men get.

I sent you my Purple Heart in a previous package, and that has a little button in the box too that you can wear in your coat lapel to show everybody how you were wounded in action. Hello, dopey.

Well, we had a wonderful time swimming yesterday, and today the whole Battalion is going swimming in the Reservoir near here. It's not safe to swim in the ocean, on account of all the mines. It's funny how all the complicated defenses face the sea, and we took them from behind. I took a lot of shots of these pill boxes and fortifications with our camera.

There was a nice poor old horse near the stone quarry. He had been wounded by shrapnel in the leg, and gangrene was setting in --- he couldn't even move --- just stood there pathetically, looking at you. I shot him with my pistol, right between the eyes. But it was the wrong place. Blood came streaming out of his nose in torrents and I put another bullet in the same place and he began prancing wildly. I wanted him to die quickly, and I put another bullet in the same place --- but he was still alive, and the blood came pouring out. One of the men who came from a farm back home then shot him from behind the ear with a German pistol, and that one must have entered his brain, because he kicked up into the air and fell over on his side. He should have been out of his pain by that time, and he died a minute or so later. I felt very unhappy about the whole thing --- I had been assured before I did it that between the eyes was the best place for a horse, but apparently it's only a cow that should be shot that way. I hesitated a long time before I pressed the trigger --- it was hard to do. He must have sensed what was happening because he kept moving his head around so that I had trouble in drawing a bead on that white spot between his eyes. And then when I finally did it the job was bungled, and he didn't die instantly as I wanted him to. After it was over, an old woman came out of a hut, and when she saw the horse lying there dead she fell on his body, sobbing and crying hysterically. This afternoon the boys are taking a nice big new horse over to her to give her in place of the poor old wounded horse that I killed so badly.

It's strange that I should have been so affected by the death of a horse when, after all, I've shot at Germans and directed Artillery fire on them, and seen them blown to bits with much personal satisfaction --- and after these things I slept well, and looked back upon the events with pleasure and a sense of accomplishment. But I felt sorry for that poor gentle old horse.

Imagine the news we just got --- oh, we're getting a rough deal, we are! For a change, we're getting a city to garrison. Wow! Usually we fight for a city, and after it's all cleaned out they move us out in the woods somewhere, and the Service Forces move in with M.P.'s and all, and the next time we try to come back there are nice big signs all over the place, "OFF LIMITS FOR TROOPS," which means combat troops of course. The chair-borne boys get the run of the place. But this time, instead of being moved to another fighting area, we're setting up in a city. Oh, where's my blouse & pinks?

You're funny with your school grades, you are. But you beat me in Chem 1 --- I only got a B. No, --- I didn't get your cable!

Hello, funny face.

Hey, I gotta go to Regiment for a meeting. See you later.

***

Sunday, Aug. 20, 1944

France

Dear Dopey:

This garrisoning a city really slays me. It makes you realize what a racket all these people have who move up behind the combat troops and take over as soon as a city is clear. Nothing to do but gas around with the civilians, but these SOS people really act important, as if they had a lot to do. I suppose it's all very necessary, but it sure is a vacation for us. You sit there in a jeep eating chow, and people pass by and say, *"Bon appetit, monsieur!"* The Colonel is now the City Commandant, and I am the self-constituted Chief of the Dreaded Ogpu. There are no shells falling, and you can take off your helmet and walk around in the sun bareheaded, until some general rides by and says, "Put that helmet on, and keep it on!" So you laugh at him and put it on. Because in combat nobody has to tell you to keep your helmet on, any more than they have to tell you to dig in. But over here wearing a helmet is like shining your shoes used to be back in the States --- spit and polish. Last night the Colonel came stamping in yelling, "Am I a combat soldier or not? They are giving brooms out down the block, and the civilians are grabbing too many brooms. 'The broom situation is getting out of hand,' they tell me. 'Get that broom situation under control!' "

As Chief of the Dreaded Ogpu I am trying to recruit some beautiful woman spies into my organization, but so far I have not been successful in my search. Incidentally, over here the people are much better dressed than they were in the province around the beachhead. This is a vacation resort district, and the standard of living was relatively high, although large sections of the city are completely destroyed. The girls look more like American girls than the English girls did, and seem quite pretty. I suppose I ought to do something about it, but I guess I'm too tired or too old, or something. So I confine myself to waving at them, and receiving a smile and a *"Bonjour, monsieur!"* in reply.

I feel very lazy and reluctant to write. I got a package from you day before yesterday, with a couple of cans of sardines (which were useful at the moment, because we had just run out of our supply of German sardines), and canned pineapple and cherries. The Colonel had just asked me if we'd "received any packages from our wife today." I told him I'd save the pineapple and cherries till we had to make a dinner of K rations, and he said, "Why save them? If we eat them now you won't have to carry them."

We live in a great big mansion near the sea. It's very nice, but there's no running water yet, or electricity. Send me more nice packages, and cookies & stuff.

Oh, about the pictures I took with the Leica. No way of developing them, so I just decided to leave them inside the camera, which I've done. You think this here war will be over soon? I'm getting awful tired of it, especially now that there's nothing to do but brood. I sure would like to go home some one of these here days. So long, funny face.

***

Monday, Aug. 21, 1944

France

Dear Dopey:

Is it raining in B'klyn? It's pouring here, and I've just been out on a wild goose chase. Now I've turned sailor. I've been churning around in a little bitty skiff, messing around with some little old islands off the coast. These non-combatant troops are always making trouble for us. They go swimming, and somebody hears a gun go off, so they start a report of enemy groups in the islands off shore, and the General gets a bee in his bonnet, and I have to turn sailor. It's fun though. The sea was very rough this morning, and the boat rocked from this crazy angle *(picture)* to that *(picture)*. I had a good time and I'm going to mess around some more tomorrow.

The mail isn't doing too well these days. I don't know why there is such a long time between my letters. I haven't gotten the one with the Sun clipping. I can't remember how often I've been writing, but I'm sure that I've been averaging a lot better than you've been receiving. Of course I usually don't get a chance during a hot situation. It's simply impossible then, until there's some sort of lull. I'm kept busy all the time --- remember we don't have an eight hour working day out here --- it's 24 hours. If there's a chance at night to get a little sleep, it's certainly too dark for writing, and you can't have lights in the front lines. On my job I'm as busy as the Battalion C.O. when we're attacking, but as soon as we're in the rear, like now, I have plenty of time, because S-2 is a purely tactical job, and involves practically no administrative responsibilities. I can't remember how long these busy tactical periods have lasted, because you lose all concept of time, and have no way of knowing whether an incident took place the day before or several days previously. But I don't think many days go by before I get a letter off, and lately I've been writing pretty regularly. But of course I may be wrong, because I can't remember exactly.

Of course I think about you, silly. I think about you all the time --- so much so that it impairs my efficiency. I can't tell you where on the map I am now, but I can always tell where I was a couple of weeks previously. I can tell you now about the fortress whose surrender I arranged. It was the fortress of St. Joseph, and was the key to the defense of St. Malo. The units on our flanks were able to advance, but this fortress, which we affectionately call The Rock, held us up for some time. It was a high cliff, with subterranean tunnels, and afforded a commanding position over the ground for miles around. But they couldn't stand our pounding, and put out the white flag just as we were about to assault it. Once we had that place, we cleaned up St. Malo in several hours, except for the Citadel and some islands. I'll tell you about it some day.

Who says I'm not marking time waiting for the war to end? Sure I am. Of course your psychological angle is harder. I wouldn't want to trade places. In fact, my only real psychological worry is worrying about your psychological worry in worrying about me. If it weren't for that I wouldn't mind the war so much. I know how you feel dopey darling, honest I do. But don't let it bother you. It's not so bad. Look at me now, for instance --- my biggest worry is what to do with Monsieur lé Jacques who was caught picking up too many sacks of cement in a warehouse that has no walls or roof anymore, and who has a permit from the Mayor of the city to do it. And my biggest gripe is that I spent 5 years studying that stupid old Latin, when I might have been learning French which I so sorely need now. I hate working through an interpreter, and although I can carry on a light conversation, especially with girls (!), any time I have to get some military info or discuss something with a French officer, I get hopelessly lost.

Please don't worry about me. I'm living on velvet. It's not like maneuvers. You think this here war will take long? Why don't those stinkers surrender? You should see the way one officer will make a bunch of unwilling soldiers continue to occupy a position which is hopelessly lost.

I wish the rain would stop. It makes you get all wet.

Just had a group of men brought in who were rounded up some distance from here. After a lot of stalling, they finally broke down and admitted that they had taken off during a fire fight --- said they just couldn't take it anymore. How men can desert that way and leave somebody else fighting the enemy is more than I can understand --- and how do they expect to get away with it? You see some strange things sometimes.

***

Tuesday, Aug. 22, 1944

France

Dear Dopey darling:

Just got three letters from you, three from my folks, and a package from them. You poor sweet kid --- I wouldn't neglect writing you for a million dollars, and I would in two seconds gladly cut the throat of the button boy who screwed up my mail to you. That was a pretty rough period --- the one during which you say you received no mail. I honestly can't remember now whether I actually wrote nothing during that time, because by now the whole thing is practically a blank in my memory. It's possible, I suppose, but if it's true I assure you it couldn't have been otherwise. However, I think the chances are that I did write, but that mail just didn't get through --- in time. You can't compare my situation with that of most of the other people you know who are overseas --- before you do, always ask whether they are Infantrymen actually in combat. You see, the great majority of men overseas are no more in combat than you are. Right now, for instance, I am in no more danger than I would be if I were riding the subway to college. Even when we get back to the Artillery positions --- which, after all, are not so far back, we consider it a vacation. Because of the fact that the Luftwaffe is practically impotent, and the enemy Artillery supply in bad condition (especially long range stuff), you don't have to go very far back to be in a nice quiet area. Sometimes even the front lines are quiet. So you see that for a person to be in France means nothing, although to you people it has tremendous connotations. What I'm getting at is that when we're in a fight it's sometimes a little difficult to get mail to the rear, while people in the rear may not have any tie-up in their mail. So in the future don't look in the mailman's sack to learn whether you ought to be getting my mail or not. It's absolutely impossible to write an equation for this sort of thing. There are too many unknowns. And don't try to make any estimates of my situation. The chances will be that you are entirely wrong.

I'm sure that by this time you've received a stack of mail. I've been writing pretty regularly for some time. I certainly have the time now, because of this silly garrison life. Last night I actually saw a double feature movie, and today I had a steak and french fried potatoes in a cafe, for 50 francs. Furthermore there's reason to think this soft deal will last a long time. Who knows, we may never see combat again. I've got enough material to write a dozen books now --- it wouldn't break my heart if those Nazi bastards surrendered tomorrow.

Now on this business of the tone of my letters. I guess maybe it did sound a little poor for a while, but you can see that my morale has been real high for some time. The period of adjustment to combat passes through many stages. You start out being very chipper and full of jokes about the whole thing, and then suddenly something happens that really shuts you up for a while. When you start talking again it's in a quieter tone of voice. Then gradually you forget and the cycle is repeated, but on a higher level. Each time you recover you consider yourself battle hardened. But actually the process is repeated many times, and it keeps forming layers of hardened scar tissue on your emotional sensitivity, until finally you can really take things in your stride. I've gotten over the period of those sad letters, dopey. You won't find me very changed. If you saw me right now I'd be practically the same guy you've always known, so let's forget those letters. That's all in the past now. It's not only true of me, but of the whole outfit. We've developed together and matured together.

I had a lovely time today. This time we really made a landing on an island. It was a beautiful day, and the sea sparkled in the sunlight. The General had ordered that we clear the island of all enemy by making an actual landing. The job was allotted to me. The Colonel promised me I could keep the island if I took it. So I'm going to mail it to you in little packages. It was so heavily mined and booby trapped that the Engineers refused to set foot on it. I knew there was no enemy on the island from having studied it through my field glasses the day before when we sailed around it. But the General had ordered that a physical reconnaissance be made. The Colonel who commanded the Port Engineer Battalion got me very sore. He told the boat crew who were to take us there that not one of them was to touch that island. "Let the combat soldiers handle it," he said. "It's not your job."

"Don't worry, Colonel," said Schmitt, our S-3, "we won't let your people go ashore." It was a rather nasty way for that Colonel to talk, especially in our presence.

Anyway, we all set out for the island in a little skiff, --- the Infantry, the Engineers, and the Navy men. When we got near the island I cast off with my little landing party in a rowboat and small motor boat. Besides myself I had my Sergeant, one of my boys, and a squad from the Regimental mine platoon. Neither the Port Engineer men nor the Navy men manned these little boats. They were piloted by two French civilian volunteers --- I guess they must have been from the Resistance --- anyway, they were damn good men.

There was also another officer, Sandler, a Jewish fellow from Texas, who was coming along just for the ride. Said he hadn't been getting enough excitement since we've been doing garrison duty. I think he's crazy. With me these things are strictly business.

The rowboat was the only craft that could make the landing. The island was solid rock jutting out of the sea, with an old French stone fortress on top. The rowboat pitched and rolled so much in the rough sea that it had me worried for a while. Sandler amused me by telling me the story of how a Nazi officer shot at him in the last battle and missed. After all the smoke cleared away the German was Sandler's prisoner. "Oh, Christ," the Nazi said. "For five whole years I've been fighting this war, and at the end of it all I get captured by a Jew!"

We found a place to make a landing, and the mine platoon boys started feeling their way carefully up the rocks. The mine detectors had become wet from the salt spray, and were of no use to us. That mine platoon sergeant was good, and I'm not kidding. I sure was glad to have him along. There was a trip wire leading to a booby trap literally every few inches we advanced up the rocks. It was a thin steel wire, close to the ground and painted to blend with the surroundings. The wire led to the safety pin on a firing cap device. If you kicked the wire it pulled the pin, releasing a plunger under the action of a spring. This detonated a charge of dynamite which was inserted in a concrete shrapnel shell. The shell was stuck into the ground by means of a stake, and also camouflaged to blend with surrounding objects. We found 28 of these little Hitler dream jobs in the approach to the fort, not counting all those in the fields around, which we never bothered with. The mine boys disarmed every one. Four of them had been exploded previously by someone or something. We had no accidents. In the next package I mail home I'll send you one of the firing cap devices. The shrapnel shell is too big and too heavy to send.

The fort had been built in 1779, and stuck way up high into the sky, not at all like these modern bunkers, which are nearly all underground. There was of course no sign of life on the island, as I could easily have told the General in advance if he had ever bothered to ask me.

"Hello two to three," I said over my radio. "There are six beautiful naked women on the island. What shall I do with them? Over."

"Hello three to two," Schmitt replied from the ship. "Check them for booby traps and wait for me to land."

After we got back to the mainland we all went and had our steak dinners in a cafe. This town hadn't been touched by the war, unlike St. Malo. The streets were full of people, and for Sandler's platoon, which was garrisoning the town, life was a veritable picnic. There were big black swastikas painted on the doors of all people who had collaborated in any way with the Nazis. These people sat sullenly in their homes or shops, and no one would so much as talk to them. The honest citizens had chosen this means of designating all traitors. For women who had slept with the Nazis, the universal treatment throughout liberated France is to shave off all their hair as a mark of disgrace. The Army civil affairs officers (a non-combat outfit) try to interfere with this system of justice. The French people can't understand the Americans. "Why are you so good to the *Boches* ?" they ask. "Don't you know what they have done to us?" They can't understand our system of handling German prisoners.

There was a strange thing in this town in connection with the Russians. I'm sure that the Germans have been using certain degenerate Russian elements in this area. They kept these men in confinement without feeding them, and then would turn them loose on the civilian population. They were like animals, and roamed the countryside, raping and pillaging. The French people came to fear them even more than they did the Germans. The Nazis used this as a means of political instruction. "You see," they would tell the French, "what kind of people are supposed to be your Allies?"

I believe I wrote you once before about the Russian diary I found in a German Battalion C.P., whose author was a White Guard pro-German

Russian. There will be an interesting story behind all this after I have pieced these things together. Clearly these "Russians" were quite different from the ones we captured, who were intelligent educated men, and had been forced into German uniform after capture on the Russian front. But I am convinced that somewheres the Germans did find degenerate or weak-minded Russian elements, and have been employing them in France.

Wed. Aug. 23, 1944

Got two more letters from you this morning, baby face --- one dated Aug. 2 and the other Aug. 15. I got a copy of that clipping from my parents too, and I am boiling mad, as you can well understand. I really ought to sue the Sun for libel if I had time for such things, although I am glad they contacted you during a period when you received no mail. I've heard of inaccurate reporting, but I never dreamed anyone could be guilty of such complete distortions. The worst parts of all were the direct quotations, which I believe must have been composed by someone back in the States, because they had no relation to anything I ever said. They simply write what they please, and put quotation marks around it.

Last night we had a reporter from the A.P. He's preparing an article for Collier's magazine on the battle of St. Malo, but I assure you he got no information from me, although, as you know, I could give him plenty of interesting facts. The Executive Officer filled him up with a lot of --- , as well as champagne and cognac. My name apparently got involved, because he wanted my address, and he said patronizingly, "You've done a good job, Baker," when he was introduced to me. "And you're going to get your name in Collier's Magazine." I guess he expected me to fall on my knees and thank him with tears in my eyes or something. So now you can start watching in Collier's for an article quoting me as saying I'm in favor of nudism, or denouncing the New Deal, or saying anything else Collier's wants me to say.

By the way, when I told my boss Col. Norris about how we took my island, he said, "Hmmm, glad you didn't get blown up. So hard to get replacements, you know." Of course I get to keep the island. I've christened it Dopey Dora Island, and someday I'll point it out to you.

Whee! Just heard we've taken Paris!

I'm sending you my Purple Heart Orders. If you've told my parents about my getting a little nick in the leg, you can give it to my father to file away for me. Otherwise you keep it, but don't lose it please. I have to keep it in my files, and Col. Norris' name is in the same order (he was hit the same day) and I want to have it as a memento.

Don't worry, darling, I haven't changed any to speak of. I thought for a while that maybe I'd lost my youth, but I've regained it. Feeling wonderful. We're city slickers now, and the battlefield is just a memory. Anyway, nothing could upset me very much any more. Yesterday we even had a USO show. What a racket we've got. I always land in a soft spot. This is easier than Grand Central Palace. So long, honeybunch.

***

Friday, Aug. 25, 1944

France

Dear Dopey:

Got three V-mail letters yesterday. Yours was dated Aug. 14. I got your Aug. 15 air mail letter the day before. Don't my letters sound O.K. again, pieface? Please don't worry so. I tell you everything I can. I'm not anywheres near Paris. I'm sitting on my unmentionable in a certain unmentionable city "guarding" it and the surrounding area. As you probably know by now, we fought for the triple city of St.-Malo -- St. Servan -- Parame, and then we were pulled out and sent to Dinard over on the other side of the Bay. The fight for Dinard was not as hard as the St. Malo scrap.

It's interesting being in a city again. The people are coming back. The Germans drove them out of here, and all who were left behind were shot. The Nazis ran around rounding up everyone they could find. They

109

had them all up against the wall --- men, women, and children --- and machine gunned them. But as soon as we moved in it was the collaborators who started dying. They had a big demonstration down the street yesterday. A Nazi stool pigeon carried a sign saying, "This man murdered eight Frenchmen by betraying them to the Gestapo." His face was rather bashed in. They shot a woman collaborator the day before too, along with three German police dogs. These French people are O.K. *Fifty-six years later I find it hard to believe my cavalier attitude toward killing. War does something to people. But then fifty-six years is a long time.*

I told one of these non-combatant Civil Affairs officers over the phone about the demonstration going on, and he said, "Oh, goodness, we'll have to have it stopped at once."

"What for?" I said.

"It's terrible," he said. "We can't have anything like that."

"Why not?" I asked.

"It's just mob rule --- that's all it is."

"It's not mob rule," I said. "They are having these people tried by the civil courts."

"Oh," he said. "That's different. I guess we can't do anything about it then."

The French told me that one of the anti-Nazis that particular man had betrayed to the Germans was his own mother.

I was over to another town yesterday to question a woman the FFI had picked up as a German agent. She was a very pretty young girl, and was picked up with an American soldier. Before the American she had been sleeping with a Russian officer. I was interested in the Russian angle, as you know. She claimed that the Russian officer had been captured at Smolensk, and tried to run away from the Germans as soon as we started moving in. She also claimed that she had never helped the

Germans, but she was lying. The citizens of the town say that the Russians were in many cases worse than the Germans, and that it didn't look like they were forced to do everything they did. The Russians in that particular area were definitely not entirely innocent victims. It seems to me that among the Russian prisoners the Germans have managed to find certain weak elements whom they were able to bully into working for them, and then trapped them little by little, saying that if the Americans ever caught them they'd be turned over to the Soviet government and shot as traitors. And they must have succeeded in breaking these people to the extent where they were so afraid that they were willing to do anything for the Germans. It's the same old game the Nazis used to play in trapping members of the underground and forcing them to betray their own people, by tricking them and getting them in deeper and deeper. I know that the Russians we ran into in combat were not of this type, and surrendered to us first chance they got, but the Russians in this area tried to hide from us. There lies an interesting story behind all this. I guess the Soviet gov't is investigating the whole thing. I believe there have been a number of Russian traitors operating in this particular area.

> *Stalin evidently was not troubled by such fine distinctions, and made a clean sweep. Everyone captured by the Germans was arrested upon coming home after the war, and sent to Siberia. He even allowed his own son to be executed by the Germans, rather than negotiate his release.*

Nothing much to write about. We are living a life of ease. Saw some crummy movie last night, and tonight we've got "Amazing Mrs. Holliday" playing. The city is coming to life too. There's a bus running, and I think before long the cafes will start opening.

Don't let that old Physics 12 throw you. It's really very easy. I sure wish I could sink my teeth into some good physics problems again. I'm getting bored with the life I'm leading. I hope it won't take much longer.

We had a discussion last night on why our soldiers don't feel the war more personally, and just sit back and let their officers go running out ahead of them while they hide in some hole or take off to the rear. The Colonel was the only one of the officers who saw the problem in the correct light, I think. The others have the idea we're just fighting for some abstractions, unlike the European people who are clearly fighting for their lives. But the way Col. Norris put it, we're fighting here so we won't have to fight in Mexico or the United States two years from now. He has a very sound perspective, instinctively, although he has been educated along the lines of the typical West Pointer. But he is one swell guy to be working for.

What I said about our soldiers is certainly not 100% true, but it has been true of a lot of the replacements. For one thing they are frightened by those phony button boys in the rear and in England who paint gruesome stories of how tough the Nazis are, and how terrible are our casualties, and frighten the poor kids to death before they ever get up here. The further you get from the front lines the more gruesome the stories get. These people, who have never seen combat, stick their chests out and talk like grizzled warriors. Somebody ought to do something to shut them up.

But our casualties were terrible, and I knew it. Or had I just decided to forget it for now?

We've already had our rear echelon loudmouths shut up. You know from my letters the caliber of the Germans we've actually run into. And we've seldom encountered such terrible ordeals that a little education wouldn't help a man survive, provided he had an average temperament. Nervous people aren't worth a damn in the Infantry. They're liable to crack in the first shelling. They just lose their minds and start blubbering and crying like children. In the last war it was called shell shock. Now the medics call it combat exhaustion. But it's simply a form of insanity due to fear and nervousness.

You ask why I don't write more letters, and everybody else says I'm always writing. "What? Are you writing that wife of yours another letter?" said the Colonel just now. But he writes a lot too --- often during a battle, if there's a lull. He always raises a big stink if the mail doesn't arrive either. That's what I like about him. He's a big chow hound too. Eats more than I do.

The Colonel has appointed me Minister of the FFI. "Baker," he says. "Put on your Minister-of-the-FFI hat." You should see me struggling with my lousy French and the Frenchmen's lousy English to arrive at an understanding. Oh, why did I have to take five years of Latin? "So talk Latin to them," says the Colonel. "Hell," I say, "I can't even talk Latin."

Mail came in, but nothing for me, dammit. Col. got three letters. He says his wife went up in an airplane and her fountain pen started leaking, so she went to have it fixed. "That's what comes of high school Physics," he said.

Hello there you.

***

Sunday, Aug. 27, 1944

France

Dear Dopey:

The chaos of victory has settled over us again, with the result that we haven't received any mail for a couple of days. So I just have to wait. I'm sending you a candid camera shot I happened to be in. It's the only picture I've got of me in France. It was taken during the battle for St. Malo. There isn't much of me to see in it, but it's better than nothing.

I had a big fight today with Schmitt, the S-3. Every once in a while I lose my patience entirely over this business of American chauvinism and get into a scrap with somebody. "I don't care if you call the Frenchmen 'frogs' privately," I said. "But it's hardly the height of diplomacy to use the expression in the presence of a French officer who understands English." Schmitt, being a particularly stupid lunkhead, took the thing personally. Everybody seems to think that all foreigners are a sort of American burden --- we're just doing the French a favor fighting the war for them. And just because their speech is peculiar and their manners different from ours, that automatically makes them freaks. I'm sick to death of that universal American viewpoint. But I guess it's not limited to Americans --- it's probably true of most peoples. And I know that many

113

of these funny little Frenchmen have killed more Germans than we've even seen.

I'll never forget the Frenchman who was giving me some information about an objective we once had to take. It was an amphibious operation, and presented some pretty tough problems. "Do you think it will be very difficult?" I asked him finally.

"Difficile, monsieur?" he said. *"C'est impossible!"*

"Rien est impossible," I told him.

"Mais oui, monsieur," he said. "In that case I will guide you there myself!"

Everywhere I go I find myself fighting the American master race psychosis. In England it was "those damned limeys," and now it's the "frogs." I liked the English, and I like the French even more. They are very frank people, and fond of their liberty, and hatred of the enemy to them is not just a lot of propaganda. They think nothing of giving their lives to free their country of the Nazis. They don't hesitate in dealing with the home-grown Fascists.

Of course they have their faults. They are always late for appointments, and like all Europeans, seem to us chaotic in their habits. And apparently unity is their biggest problem. I have learned that the FFI is not the only partisan organization. Among others there is the FTP, which I am told is the Communist organization. My friend Lt. Arvengas, of the De Gaulle Army, is very concerned about the danger of revolution. He says practically every Frenchman now has a weapon, and that although the FTP did very good work against the Nazis, he is afraid of them now. "But I thought all these organizations are supposed to be united under de Gaulle," I said. "They are supposed to be," he told me.

Yesterday I had business in Rennes, which was a pretty long trip. That's quite a city. It's the first city of that size I've seen in France, and it really is something. It hasn't been hit by the war, and the streets are full of people, and the stores are all open. I bought you a little pair of black earrings which I thought would look pretty on you, and I'm mailing them to you, together with the firing mechanism on one of the booby traps I wrote you about. I'm tired of sending you war souvenirs all the time, and the earrings will be my first non-tactical gift to you from France. The camera is a war trophy, and the booby trap a memento of a rather interesting morning, but the little black earrings are just a present to my dopey wife. Wait till I get to Paris. Then I'll have to get you something really nice.

***

Monday, Aug. 28, 1944

Dear Dopey:

I'm going to try to send you a better picture, but this is all I have now. I'm the guy in the middle. Of course I'm not blowing up a balloon, silly. I'm talking over the radio. I'm sorry I ain't better looking. *C'est la vie*. It's strictly an unposed picture. Baker at work.

Now you send me one. But please look nicer than I do. (How could you help it?)

***

Tuesday, Aug. 29, 1944

France

Dear Dopey:

Got two dehydrated letters from you today, viz., V-mail. But they were typed, so you had enough room to say more than hello or goodbye. The dates were Aug. 16 & 17. I think I've gotten most of your letters, but there are a couple of things which are new to me in your summary --- Carl's being busted, "nobody" knows why, and I infer that Marty Greenberg is K.I.A.

You know what I'm doing right now? We are all sitting in a room which has been blacked out, and we have a light attached to a battery. It's 10 P.M. We are grouped around a table --- the Colonel and staff, and there are six bottles on the table --- cognac, wine, gin, and God knows what else. And in the middle is a box of my Aunt Mania's *hoomentaschen.* I could have your two cans of pineapples and cherries, but they're in my jeep out at the motor pool and it's too much trouble to get them. But everybody is drinking out of the bottles and eating Aunt Mania's cookies, and exchanging battle yarns. I will probably be slightly drunk by the end of this letter, but don't let that bother you, funny face.

Wow, would I like to see you in that zippy red bathing suit. Please send me some pictures, darling, huh? In technicolor, maybe?

Don't know what to write about --- nothing ever happens to me. Wish the war would end so I could sink my teeth into some exciting math problems again.

We are discussing the way people snore. "There is nothing so disconcerting," says the Colonel, "as sleeping in the same foxhole with a man who snores."

Now we're comparing notes on what a coincidence it is that every time you crawl out of a hole to take a leak, no sooner do you get your unmentionable out than the enemy starts shelling again and you have to jump back in your hole. You can't imagine how annoying this is apt to become, if continued over a long period of time. Or --- when the shelling starts several people are standing near the same foxhole, and everybody knocks everybody else down in the mad scramble to get in, and six people try to squeeze into the same hole, and they hold down their hats and say, "I beg your pardon. Excuse me, excuse me!" But most of our most recent fighting has been in populated areas and cities, and it hasn't been necessary to dig in, because of the shelter provided by these nice substantial French houses.

All this is in the past anyway. It's been so long since we've done any fighting that we've practically forgotten how it feels to hear the whine of a shell or crack of a bullet over your head. We're strictly garrison soldiers now.

I hope you have a nice vacation, baby, darling. I sure would like to spend it with you. You think you can get an afternoon off, or an extended lunch our, or something, when I come home?

It's getting late, and the bottles are nearly empty, and the cookies are about gone. Gee, I can't tell what the hell I'm drinking --- everything on the bottles is written in French.

Me, I'm going to bed. Let's both go to bed.

Somebody went and spilled a whole bottle of something all over the letter, so I had to readdress the envelope.

"Wow, do I wanna see my baby wife," I said.

"Oh, you and your wife!"

"Aaah!"

"Nyaah!"

"Oh, you and your wife!"

***

Sept. 1, 1944

France

Dear Dopey-face:

The mail is screwed up something terrible. I did get a package of yours today (sent to old address), but you people always use such crumby boxes that they're always about to fall apart.

Hey! You're starting your vacation today. You going to that dude ranch? How is Sherry and her toe? Is she getting the Purple Heart too?

I guess I don't know how lucky I am to get to spend my summer vacation in France. We've had nothing of the heat spell you had in New York. There hasn't been a single uncomfortably hot day all summer.

117

There were a few times when things got kind of hot, but that wasn't the weather. The last couple of weeks I've been living in a strictly vacation district too. People used to come here to spend the summers in the days before the beaches were lined with barbed wire and *"Achtung -- Minen"* signs. The people have been streaming back, and already ferry-boats are crowded with passengers, the streets are filled with bicycles, and couples walk down the boardwalk along the water's edge.

I just found out why we haven't gotten our mail. The latest snafu by the button boys --- they sent our mail to Paris --- which does us a lot of good; --- they might just as well send it to Brooklyn.

I've been having a good time lately, but I can't tell you about it yet. Next letter I write, it won't be military info any more, I think. Jesus Christ, if I actually break into print every time one of those phony war correspondents asks me how to spell my name and what my address is, I don't see where they'll find room for war headlines.

I just drank a can of condensed milk, and we've been eating your chocolate wafers that I got today, as well as the can of pears. Everybody thinks I'm crazy because I drink condensed milk straight. Do you think I'm crazy?

I see from my parents' letter that you told them about how I stopped some shrapnel. I suppose it doesn't matter much, anyway. I can't imagine how much they worry about me. I can remember how they used to worry if I spent a night away from home, or got my feet wet, or something like that. If they worry in the same proportion now, their imaginations must be conjuring up far worse pictures than the reality presents. So your telling them could do no harm. My scratch wasn't even worth mentioning, it was so trivial. This Army gives medals for the damndest things.

***

Sunday, Sept. 3, 1944

France

Dear Dopey:

Finally sweated out a letter from you. It's stamped Aug. 24, but dated by you Aug. 14. You've certainly got plenty of news. I see that practically everybody's pregnant except us. I guess we'll have to do something about that when I get home. We always get there, you know, even if it is a little later than other people. After all, breeding is only one of our activities. Other people have more time.

The war is over for Carl, apparently. I sure hope they do a good repair job on him. He should be flown in. A case of his type requires immediate treatment. Give Sherry my love, and tell her that the medics are doing really good work on people. Actually he's very lucky. I've seen men bleed to death with that artery cut before they could get proper attention. He must have been pretty close to an Aid Station when he was hit.

I have a feeling that the war is damn near over for me too, but for a very different reason. We're so far to the rear now, and things are moving to such a rapid conclusion that I doubt very much if we'll ever see combat again. There was an island still holding out, and we just pounded the living hell out of it. They had practically nothing to shoot back with, and it was a great holiday for the French civilians, who lined the waterfront and watched the *Boches* get a taste of their own medicine. We were holding amphibian maneuvers with assault boats, and drawing maps and taking photographs to brief the troops for the landing. Just as we were about to assault the island with our landing craft, and at the very moment when the Battalion Commander was issuing the attack order, the bastards hoisted the white flag. They couldn't stand it anymore. The German officers always have an excuse for surrendering. This one told us that he just couldn't stand living with the Italians any more. They were driving him crazy. It was a little disappointing in a way. It sure would have been good training. The only amphibious operations I've been in to date have been dry runs.

This must have been pure bravado. It was easy enough to talk that way once it was all over. There is no way I could ever have welcomed an amphibious assault just to get the experience.

But I suppose it's really for the best. If they had been at all determined they could have cost us plenty of lives. I've never forgotten the lesson of Stalingrad. In the last analysis only Infantry can drive out a determined foe. This joker was the nearest thing to being determined I've run into. I made a couple of trips out there before our D-day to negotiate. He kept saying that he couldn't surrender because it was against orders.

But after each pounding he became more nervous, and began bargaining for terms. Then he said he would radio for permission to surrender and would put out the white flag if permission was granted. Only Hitler himself could give him this permission, he said. When he walked away, a non-com lagged behind and whispered to us, "Come back even if there's no white flag. We'll surrender anyway." This was the first violation of discipline I've had occasion to observe in the German Army before capture. Usually they're more scared of the officers than of us. Well, there was no white flag at the prescribed time, but we went back to the island anyway. The officer said that he hadn't been given permission to surrender, but that he would let those men who wanted to give up do so the next morning. Meanwhile things became very tense on the island. A large body of men started to crowd around one spot with their overcoats and all, ready to be taken back to the mainland. There was a distinct cleavage, most of the men joining the group which was insisting on surrender, while others held back. I thought sure there would be some shooting pretty soon, but it never happened. We left them to think it over, and resumed shelling.

When the white flag went up the next morning, we tore out there in our assault boats. The sea was real rough, and we were completely drenched by the time we got there. The island was just a mass of rubble. There wasn't an inch of ground that hadn't be shelled or bombed. But the underground bunkers still had not been destroyed, and most of the men were still alive. Of course their big guns were knocked out. But if they had really been determined, and not afraid to die, they could have brought their machine guns out as soon as we approached the island to storm it and our Artillery fire lifted --- it would have been a rough party. But they chose surrender --- the officer couldn't control them.

We found Russians out there too. Here's my final judgment on this Russian business: The Germans capture them on the Russian front, torture and starve them, as they do all Russian prisoners. When they're half starved and nearly beaten to death, the Germans announce, "We're going to give you people an opportunity to get some decent food and a good life. All you have to do is join the German Army." They promise them that they'll never be sent anywhere near the front, and will be used for non-combatant jobs only. The weaker ones give in, and once they're caught the Germans can do anything they want with them, because they inform them that the Russians regard them as traitors, --- which they are --- and then these miserable souls become men without a country. They were of little use to the Germans as fighters, but they were used for garrisoning forts and cities, and on jobs where they could be watched. But the situation developed so rapidly that these troops were swept up and tossed into the melee.

With the Russian officers, it's a different story. There haven't been many, but there have been some. Maybe a few of them have been weaklings too, but I believe that in the case of at least some there was a political element involved, and I'm sure that some White Guard emigrés are being used by the Germans.

Anyway, the Russians sure do start tovarishching me when they find I speak Russian. They will have a lot of questions to answer after the war. I think it's just that they couldn't take it. Of course there are a number of Russians who were forced to work for the Germans, but I'm talking about combat troops. The Nazis are masters at the art of demoralizing and breaking an individual. You know how they used to work on the German underground. All a man has to do is give in a little, and they've got him trapped.

Of course the Germans hate their guts, and vice versa. And they seldom put up anything of a scrap. It's this kind of element which is contributing to the collapse of the *Deutsche Wehrmacht*. The Nazis are being caught in their own noose.

Yesterday a Captain and I went over to a certain city to set up a Company there. I had a couple of my boys along, and they got involved with three French women. Two of them looked all right too. It's been a long time since I've gotten to talk to a pretty girl. These were trying to talk us into coming home with them. "Too windy *pour le promenade,"* they said. You come weath we, yes?"

I thought they were professionals, but as it turned out they weren't. They just loved all Americans, that's all. The boys asked if they couldn't have a half hour off. "Take an hour," I said. The Captain and I still had some business, and we agreed to meet at the end of an hour. They pulled a bottle of rum out of the jeep, and off they went.

An hour later there was no sign of them. So we set out to track them down. The house was near by. We described them to civilians, who directed us to the house. It turned out to be a nice chateau with two pianos. According to law everyone is allowed to occupy a house until the owner returns. There are so many houses destroyed that rooming space can't be wasted, so everybody just picks a house and moves in.

The boys had accomplished their mission, but were still feeling pretty high, as were the girls. After I tasted some of that rum I could see the reason why. That stuff was potent. So were the girls. "You killed *Boche?"* asked the blonde.

"Oui."

"Oh, that good! Good! The *Boche* no good." She turned out to be Polish. I spoke Russian to her, and she replied in Polish, and it amazed me that we could actually understand each other. Her brother had been killed by the Germans, as well as her sweetheart. She had been thrown into jail for slapping a Nazi officer in the face, and I gathered that the Germans then brought her to Paris into forced prostitution (although she didn't actually say so. She said they sent her to work in a factory. I guess it amounted to the same thing in the end anyway).

All the girls insisted on telling their stories, and why they hated the *Boches.* "You kill many *Boches?"* they would ask, and if you said, *"Oui,"* they would throw their arms around you and kiss you, murmuring, "Oh, that good! Good!." And they would turn to another soldier and repeat the process.

However, I managed to remain a good boy (believe it or not), and we finally tore ourselves away, although they climbed all over the jeep, saying, "I come visit you tomorrow, and we sleep together till Monday."

I asked the boys, "Did you at least use some rubbers?"

"No, sir," they said. "We didn't have any, and they looked pretty clean, anyway."

"For Christ sakes," I said. "You know we've got plenty of German rubbers in the jeep."

***

So old Irv Heymont is a Major, no less. His address sounds like he's landed some soft job at the Infantry School too. I think his Army career will be a great success. *My friend Irv had gone into the Regular Army before war broke out.* It's too bad he hasn't had some combat experience though. I'd rather have my experience than his rank, but a Majority is nothing to sneeze at. Send him my regards and tell him to write me first. After all, with all that rank he's got, how can I open the correspondence? It would be almost presumptuous. However, if I'm not too lazy, maybe I will.

Now I'm going for a swim at that same pool where I took the pin-up pictures.

Enjoy your vacation, funny face. Send pictures, *s'il vous plait.* I love you too.

***

(Published in March, 1945 *Infantry Journal*) Sunday, Sept. 1944

France

Dear Irv:

Sitting around a table here in France batting the breeze the conversation got around to how does the real thing differ from the dry runs back in the States. And since you've landed at Benning, I thought you might be interested in the observations of a humble lieutenant who has just completed two months of combat.

Mortars. Mortars have played a much more important role than they ever could have in maneuvers. In hedgerow fighting we attached forward observers to front-line companies, the same as artillery forward observers, and we kept on using this system after we got out in the open.

Instead of the precision system of calculation that was used in training, the FO simply calls for fire at certain coordinates --- it's very hard to do arithmetic when somebody is shooting at you. He then adjusts fire the same way as for artillery.

Artillery in close support. Artillery and mortar fire produce more casualties than small arms, and the artillery is the infantry's biggest weapon. Usually the liaison officer goes with the battalion CO in the OP group, and FOs are attached to each of the front line companies. As soon as the company is held up by MG or other fire, the company CO merely calls for fire and in a minute or two it comes down. The battery OP system has been used only once in my experience and that was in a recent operation on an island which was holding out and which we reduced by artillery and air bombardment. At the very moment when the battalion CO was issuing the attack order for the assault with landing craft the Krauts hoisted the white flag. But outside of that situation, when fire on the island would be controlled from the mainland, we've never used the battery OP system. It was particularly impractical in hedgerow fighting when you couldn't see more than 200 yards in front of you. If the FO becomes a casualty the infantry directs the fire. I had a hell of a big time directing fire on a big gun firing from the Citadel. We actually picked up the flash of the gun with a captured German BC scope.

Tanks and TDs in support. The school solution was that tanks must always be employed in mass, but here it's been the practice to attach a platoon of tanks or TDs to an infantry battalion which has run into resistance. But you have to be careful not to let the tanks get way out ahead or sure as hell they get knocked out by AT guns or bazookas. The infantry and tanks give mutual support. They move together. I'll never forget the day we wangled ourselves a platoon of tanks and lost four out of five of them in two minutes. They tore down the road in column at such a clip that the infantry couldn't keep up with them, and they were knocked out before you could say boo. But they can't be beat for cleaning up machine guns when the infantry gets pinned down and can't move forward. In the hedgerow fighting it was usually necessary to blow gaps in the hedges with bangalore torpedoes before we could throw in the armor.

Cover. On maneuvers we always used to get skinned because we stuck our heads up too much and never crawled. In combat you never have to tell a man to get down --- the biggest problem is making him get up. As soon as he gets some fire he hits the ground. The Germans had it doped out. They put their machine guns so as to hold us up at a certain hedgerow. They had their mortars and artillery zeroed in on this hedgerow and as soon as we'd stop, down it came. That's how we got our heaviest casualties. Our job in that situation was to sell the idea that the men stood a much better chance if they kept moving forward than if they stopped. And that's a fact. I'd much rather keep attacking day after day than stop and sweat out the artillery fire.

You don't have to tell a man to dig when he should dig, either. Dig or die --- it's as simple as that, and everyone knows it right off the bat. Until we got into the populated districts and street fighting, our shovels were as important as our rifles.

Small arms. The carbine is a damned good weapon if it's kept properly cleaned and oiled. But I don't care how much you people talk about care and cleaning of equipment, it's a physical impossibility to keep that carbine clean enough to function in combat. As soon as you hear the whine of a shell and hit the ground, your weapon is dirty again and jams. But the M1 can't be beat. You can drag it through mud (and you do) and it keeps on firing. I'm a battalion staff officer and I got rid of my carbine as soon as I could get hold of a tommy gun and a pistol.

I got rid of it a lot sooner than that. Within a couple of days I was carrying an M1, of which there was an abundance, left over from casualties. Tommy guns were a lot harder to come by.

But I found that the tommy gun slows me up and I carry it only when I go on motorized patrols or independent missions. Otherwise the pistol is enough in case of an emergency. Practically every man in the outfit has a pistol by now --- mostly German.

A rifle, too, may jam, and it's good to have something else to fall back on. Also, you might lean your rifle up against a tree and walk off, but your pistol is always strapped to your waist.

Enemy information. I was a battalion S-2 on maneuvers and rarely had much to do. It's a different story in combat. The S-2 moves with the OP and works very closely with the battalion CO. There have been times when the battalion would be held up and I've gotten the exact location of the enemy positions from a prisoner and brought artillery fire down on them, enabling the battalion to advance. Once I got a Kraut sergeant of an engineer battalion to point out the fields where his battalion was bivouacked, and we shelled them all night with light and medium artillery. I talk to the prisoners before they have cooled off and start remembering that name-rank-and-serial-number business. There is a tendency to underestimate the enemy as a result of prisoner information and you have to make correction for the prisoner's demoralization. My knowledge of German has come in pretty handy.

Travel light. On maneuvers we had packs, musette bags, and all kinds of junk. Here all we carry is weapons, ammo, shovel, and canteen. I don't even wear suspenders --- just the pistol belt. The shovel, pistol, ammo and canteen are hooked to the belt. I started out with a fancy map board but I soon found that I would get all tangled up in it --- besides, it draws fire. Now I just fold up the map and stick it in my shirt.

The psychological element. On maneuvers we could say that a unit was pinned down, which meant that they couldn't more forward. Here when a unit is pinned down it means that men are dying. You can find a mask of ground to protect you from small-arms fire, but it's little protection against artillery and mortar fire. Too often the men will just lie there while their officers or non-coms run out ahead of them and get killed because they're all alone. Then the unit has no leader. Green replacements lack confidence and as they're moving up to the front they hear all kinds of gruelling stories at rear echelon about how they'll be dead within two days and how tough the enemy is.

The less a man has seen of combat the more gruesome the picture he paints. Once we silenced these cooks and clerks in the rear, we found that the men were arriving in much higher spirits. Yet they still keep asking whether they're at the front, and every time a gun goes off they jump into a ditch. But they soon catch on and learn how to tell when a shell is coming or going, and if they can only be sold on the need for aggressiveness they're all right. The caliber of officers has been exceptionally and consistently high. As I told you, very often the platoon leader turns around and finds that he's left his men far behind. This has cost us a lot of good officers.

I notice I don't tell him what our casualty rates were. This would have to wait for a letter to be written many years later. He showed the above letter to his Regimental C.O., who directed that it be read to all troops and posted on bulletin boards. The Division Commanding General reacted similarly. But the Corps Commander picked up on the item disparaging the carbine, and ordered the letter banned and all copies destroyed, whereupon Irv sent it to the Infantry Journal, which published it as an article in March, 1945, entitled "It's a Tough Racket." They couldn't find me to get permission, so they signed it Lieutenant Ohio after my Division, which was called the Ohio Division, and sent a check that reached me at the hospital in England. When I read the article now, the breezy style makes it sound like maneuvers. Was I just trying to be "professional," or was it an attempt to keep up morale? I knew we had to win this war, and one was not likely to get enthusiastic recruits for a suicide job.

***

Monday, Sept. 4, 1944

France

Dear Dopey:

I just wrote you a letter last night, but I've got to tell you about the new place we moved into today. It must have cost around 20 bucks a day to stay in this chateau in peace time. It's the most beautiful place I've ever seen, and glory of glories --- running water! And toilets that flush! Every officer has a room with a bed. Mine has a big double window with a view to the ocean, which you can hear roaring against the rocks below. We're going to eat our meals out of plates too. I don't know how long we'll be here, but it sure will be good while it lasts.

I got a letter from you today dated Aug. 19 and stamped on the outside Aug. 18. Why don't you and the postal people get together? ... The postal people don't discriminate against the lower grades, --- they --- up everybody's mail they can. Apparently a stack of our mail is still floating around Paris, but we're getting the more recent mail. The Colonel gets sore as hell when he gets no mail --- says he'll just refuse to fight if it doesn't come through.

I've gotten so many packages lately that I've accumulated a lot of canned goods which I haven't had a chance to eat. In combat, when you have to live on K rations, that stuff comes in real handy, but now I don't get much chance to eat it.

I'm not at all surprised that silly McGowan got himself captured. When I saw him he was about to barrel down the St. Lô-Périers highway, till we told him that it was still in enemy hands. These correspondents seldom show themselves at the front lines when there's any shooting going on, but they often blunder into something. There's a lot of confusion during a fast moving situation, and these people get very mixed up. Remember reading about the naval convoy that was ambushed on the way to St. Malo? St. Malo was in enemy hands at the time, and these people, strictly non-combat troops, were on their way there to do some port construction work. They rode down a nice quiet road, when suddenly they found themselves surrounded by German tanks and were wiped out by machine gun fire. I came down the same road a couple of hours later, and was stopped by French civilians who told me what had happened. I waited there for the Battalion to come up, and they detrucked and deployed outside the road and pushed the Germans back. The next morning we found the Navy men there by the road dead. Often there are places where you can cross over to the enemy lines without hearing a shot fired --- like the time I entered a village which was still occupied by the Germans.

I am feeling fine. I still love you, and the longer we go without doing any fighting, the more restless I get, and the more anxious to get home. I told my driver Smitty to paint your name on the jeep, and yesterday he got hold of some white paint and stenciled it on. I meant for it to be in only one place, but I found DOPEY printed all over the jeep in big letters --- so every time I get into the jeep I think of you. Maybe it will bring me luck too, I bet.

I got a letter from Rivkie today too. She says she wants to go to Hawaii, and that all the girls who went to California with her have gone home leaving her feeling rather lonesome. She doesn't feel that she ought to go home till the war is over. I think I'll answer her now. ... Have a good vacation, dopey. I'm having one.

***

Monday, Sept. 4, 1944

France

Dear *(sister-in-law)* Rivkie:

I've got it real soft these days, and it's weeks since we've done any real fighting. We almost had to storm an island that was holding out, but just as we were about to take off they hoisted the white flag. They couldn't stand our Artillery and aerial pounding --- unlike the fighters of Stalingrad. The Germans are getting a wonderful dose of their own medicine now. Their whole Blitzkrieg is being repeated in reverse. This time it's we who have complete superiority of everything --- and they can't take it. Right now I'm living in a beautiful French chateau on the edge of the sea. You can hear the wind and the breakers pounding the rocks below. This is beautiful country, and you'd like it very much here. Yesterday I went swimming in a fresh water pool nearby. It seems like a long time since I've heard the whine of a shell when it's heading your way and you're sure that this one really has your number on it. The last letter I wrote you caught me in an unpleasant mood, and isn't at all typical of the way I've been feeling. You make some kind of adjustment to combat, and after a while you don't mind it so much. And things have been going quite well for us. It's the Germans who are doing the dying now. Only when you're not fighting you get very restless and anxious to be home again.

The French are making short shrift of the collaborators. The universal treatment is first to parade them through the streets for all to see and then line them up against the wall, perhaps along with some German dogs, and shoot them. The homes of all people who showed any friendship for the Nazis have black swastikas painted on them, so that all may know. The women who slept with the Nazis have their hair shaved off. Incidentally, there are quite a few of these. In some cases we found them inside bunkers along with the Nazis, and when we drove the Nazis out the women came out with them. I have a great deal of affection for the French, who are wonderfully frank and direct people, and know how to take care of traitors. I get into a lot of fights with our people, who insist on calling them frogs and displaying the same contempt for "foreigners" which is so typical of our countrymen. The usual argument is, "If they had been on the ball we wouldn't have had to come here in the first place. ... They're no good. We ought to give them back to the Germans, etc., etc." To Americans everybody who is different with respect to language or customs is a screwball. But I suppose other people are the same way, only I get to see it more in the case of the Americans.

I think your taking every course that comes up is a swell idea --- and going to Hawaii will be a good experience for you. People are really needed out there. But make sure that you won't get stuck there after the war is over. There are plenty of good jobs and necessary ones for you in the States. I don't believe the Pacific war will last very long after the

European war is concluded. ... What's superhets? I'm just a poor old ignorant Infantryman, you know. I guess it means superheterodynes. Or is it superhepcats?

Your experience with sailors is pretty typical. You often see sailors involved in scraps like that, while for soldiers it's rather unusual. Our Navy, besides being the most reactionary of the armed forces, is also the most undisciplined. Sailors when off duty are like a bunch of animals turned loose. It's not true of all of them, of course, and in all cases it's the fault of the naval authorities, who encourage this sort of action by refusing to punish offenders. They seem to think that this roughens them up and makes them good fighting men. It's too bad they can't spend a little time in the front lines with the Infantry, if they're so full of fight. In towns run over by sailors it isn't safe for a girl to walk around alone at night. Dora had a rather unpleasant experience one night on Utica Avenue with two sailors, and was nearly scared to death. It gets me sore as hell. I've heard of cases where the Navy has refused to try men in cases of rape. They just choose to overlook it.

Somebody brought in three Russians this afternoon. They had been sent into forced labor in Germany and then in France, and were picked up by our men because they thought they might be German soldiers in civilian clothes. We've captured a lot of Russians in German uniforms. The Germans have actually succeeded in bludgeoning some soldiers captured on the Russian front into joining the German Army by starving and torturing them. But these men I got this afternoon were merely forced laborers. ... I've captured Russian officers of as high a grade as Lt. Col. I will say this for them --- these Russians have never put up a decent fight. There was a Russian Battalion in this area, and they surrendered en masse in the first battle. So far I've had Poles, Russians, Dutch, Yugoslavs, and Italians. The German Army is in sad shape.

Give my love to America. So long Rivkie.

***

Around Wed., Sept. 6, 1944

France

Dear dopey baby:

I got your Aug.18 V-mail last night in the middle of a big blowout we were having for Company Commanders and Staff. We had steak and French fries and millions of things to eat and drink. You should have seen us sitting there at a long table in a great luxurious dining hall eating and drinking, telling bawdy stories, and talking about all the crazy things that have happened to us. We had a Quartermaster Officer with us, and he started telling us how once when he was working with the Infantry he had to go five days without changing his clothes or bathing. This nearly brought the house down, because everyone sitting at the table had gone at least a month at one time or another without even getting his shoes off.

"Well, let me tell you something," he finally said after everybody quieted down again. "If you think driving a fleet of trucks down the road all night in complete blackout is easy, let me disillusion you."

"Hell," I said. "That's nothing. Did you ever try getting on the Lexington Avenue subway during rush hours?"

You write cute letters. I read your V-mail letter around eight times this morning. I had nothing else to do. Each morning we ask ourselves what we ought to do during the coming day --- go for a boat ride, go swimming, or just stay in and read. This morning I just lay in bed and kept reading your letter. I also finished "Thunder on the Left," by Chris Morley. Imagine --- I've actually read a book again. I never thought my mind would settle that much. ...

This is so much like being on vacation that it sort of wows me. Each of us has a room with bath. (Actually it's only a douche bath --- we had a hell of a time figuring out what those things were --- do you urinate in it, wash clothes in it, or use it for prophylactic stations? --- Finally we learned it's for a douche. Every room in this chateau has one.)

Yesterday afternoon I felt very restless and unhappy. I wouldn't mind a nice vacation with you over here, but the way things are my conscience is beginning to bother me. I haven't got a damn thing to do, and after all the war isn't over. It's not that I enjoy being in combat --- I've seen enough of that to last a while. --- But this goldbricking demoralizes me. I've got a lot of things to do back home, and if they don't use me for fighting I'd like to take the first boat back. There seem to be very strong rumors about our being used as occupation troops. Already our boys are patrolling the streets with MP painted on their helmets. I'd much rather we killed some more Germans and got home that much sooner. My job is one that concerns itself strictly with the enemy. When there's no enemy I have nothing to do, and after a while I start going whacky. In a sense I was much happier when we were in combat.

I would get to eat those words.

It was funny last night --- we who only a few short weeks ago were crouching in holes like animals --- sitting at a palatial banquet in a mansion as if we were kings. It seems so unreal.

Nobody understands why I write so much. It kind of annoys people a little. "What in the world do you have to write about?" they keep asking. It seems to everyone that that's all I ever do. Wow, pretty soon it'll be time to go back down to that banquet room and be served dinner --- and it seems like I just finished breakfast. We've set up a regular Officers' Mess, just like back in garrison. The Colonel can't get used to that long table. His chair is at the head of the table, and every once in a while he runs down to the other end, sits down, and yells, "What d'you say? What d'you say? I can't hear you." He had a big office with a desk set aside for himself, with telephone and all, but he's never entered it once. He likes to be where there are people and there's lots of noise going on. How will we ever get used to peacetime living again?

I just went for a motor boat ride in a launch the Chaplain found. We took some pictures too. I'll send them to you as soon as I can.

I'm awfully bored. I kind of think maybe I'd like to be around Luxembourg, or some place like that, where all the big doings are.

Give my love to Larry & Bernie. Wish I could see them. It's true I don't get ice cream sodas, but I doubt if you people get all the Vin Rouge and champagne and cognac and everything that I do.

Yet, French girls are pretty --- much more so than the English. Three Russian civilians, who had been sent into forced labor here from Russia two years ago, told me that Russian girls are even prettier. You're prettier than everybody. These three Russians were picked up by our men and turned over to me. I couldn't decide what to do with them, so I put them up overnight with the Company. The next morning when I sent for them they were nowheres around. When finally located they were doing calisthenics with the anti-tank platoon. Another couple of days and they'd have been absorbed into the outfit.

Sorry there's nothing interesting to write about. Nothing ever happens to me.

***

Thur., Sept. 7, 1944

France

Dear Dopey:

I'm enclosing an article from Yank magazine. I'd like you to keep it for me because of the towns mentioned. I'll probably never forget them as long as I live. In spite of the writer's naivete (you can see he was never up with the front line units), he has a few good things in the article, like his comparison of the Infantry to the proverbial tortoise, who moves so slowly, yet is the first to get there. From the remarks and quotations (like the one about how "unpleasant" a foxhole is --- actually a foxhole is the most wonderful thing in the world), it is evident that the troops interviewed were supply personnel or Regimental CP personnel. To a correspondent a Regimental CP is the front lines, while to front line troops it's a rest area. It's funny --- all my life I've been reading newspapers and periodicals, and although I professed disbelief, I realize now that subconsciously I must have actually put a lot of faith in what I read, because now that I'm the protagonist instead of the audience I am amazed to see how little of what is written is the writer's personal observation. He writes it as though he were "there" (he probably thinks he was), but he's actually just writing what others tell him, and those others are usually the last people he ought to be interviewing. Before I joined my outfit I too was under the illusion that every casualty in our ranks is the result of 88 mm. fire. The only people we in the rear were able to talk with were the supply personnel who came scampering to the rear as soon as they dropped their supply at a dump, and who are the least equipped to inform anyone accurately. When I got to the front I found that everything from a hand grenade to a thunderstorm is called an 88, and it always amuses us to listen to the legend that has been built around this very effective but far from omnipotent German weapon. Actually I'd say that only twice have we ever been shelled by 88's. The usual incoming mail is either mortar or 105 mm. howitzer. It was an 81 mm. mortar that got me my Purple Heart.

No mail for me last night --- sad disappointment --- better luck tonight, I hope.

I am getting more and more restless. I was happier when we were fighting. I had a job --- I did it fairly well --- people respected me for it. Now I have nothing to do but arrange movies for the men (we saw "Follow the Boys" today). I don't like Army life except when we're in combat. Then everything has meaning. Now people get on my nerves. You often have to live with people in the Army with whom you'd never associate in civilian life. Now in combat these people are different. Some of the biggest zhlubs sometimes do such wonderful things that you love them for it, while in garrison they seem like awful heels. Sometimes I wonder why some people do such heroic things in combat. They seem to have no understanding of the war and their reasons for fighting or hatred of the enemy seem petty things. Yet in action they are remarkable. There must be an intuitive political understanding. Maybe they just talk tough, but are fine people underneath. What do you think? At any rate, I like them better in combat.

Sandler is a swell guy. He's the Jewish boy from Texas who went along with me on the booby trapped island. He told me today that his inactivity is getting him down. He doesn't like sitting on his butt while other men are fighting. But everybody else seems delighted with our set-up.

Sandler was one of those who actually did understand the war. And he was the only man I ever knew who was completely without fear. "It doesn't matter what you do," he told me. "On Rosh Hashonah it's written, and on Yom Kippur it's sealed." And so apparently it was for him. I have no memory of how he died, only that one day he was gone.

8 *ANGERS*

I hated combat patrols. They just seemed a way of getting people killed, --- unlike reconnaissance patrols, which were necessary and important. One particular combat patrol I had to send out turned out to test me on a matter of principle.

It was a quiet day --- I believe it was around Dinard --- and I had a visit from a General. It was real nice to get a lull in the fighting, but the downside was that it always brought out the brass. That was when they got their medals for "exposing" themselves to enemy fire. This particular General found me because I was in charge of patrolling for the Battalion.

"What's a good German?" he asked me.

"A dead German," I replied, repeating the mantra I knew he wanted to hear.

He patted me on the back. "Here's what I want you to do. There is an enemy tank park," he said, pointing to his map and showing me the coordinates. "At 10 o'clock tonight I want you to send out a combat patrol with bazookas, and when they get there have them blow up those tanks."

"Yes, sir," I said. And he was gone.

There were several things wrong with the plan. It was a couple of miles to the tank park, and the patrol would have to get through a lot of enemy soldiers. It was a cloudy day, and would be pitch dark by 10 o'clock. I had led night patrols, and it was the scariest experience of my life. I evolved my own plan for dealing with this problem. I would send the patrols out when it was dusk, and they could still see. By the time they reached the enemy position they would have cover of darkness, but the terrain was no longer unfamiliar and they could at least find their way back.

So I sent the patrol out at 8 o'clock, figuring they should reach the tank park around 10 o'clock, if they ever got there, which was doubtful. At 8:30 there was a message from Regiment informing me that at 9 o'clock there would be a Corps Serenade called down on the tank park, to soften it up for the mission. In a Corps Serenade all the artillery of an entire Army Corps is fired at a single target. The patrol should still be nowhere near there at 9 o'clock, but it was an unbelievable amount of fire power, and stray shells would be landing all over the place.

It was real bad news. If any of those men were lost as a result, it was something I would have to live with the rest of my life. But if I called off the Serenade, I would have to admit I had disobeyed a direct order from a General. He would be furious. I had ruined his beautiful plan. What was the use of being a General if a 1st Lieutenant could disregard his orders? He would have me court martialed. I didn't know what the sentence would be, but I would be finished as far as the Army was concerned.

On the other hand if I just sat it out, it was not so different from the kind of close artillery support we sometimes got in an attack, which always ran some risk of casualties from friendly fire. Anyway, chances were the patrol would never get that far. They would run into enemy troops, maybe exchange some fire, and get the hell out. Or, as I knew sometimes happened in such cases, they would sit under a tree and then come home saying they couldn't find the objective, which was not entirely untrue. Calling off the Corps Serenade was asking for trouble, and for nothing.

I turned the crank on the field telephone and rang up Regiment. "You'll have to call off the Corps Serenade," I said. "The patrol went out at 8 o'clock, and I can't call them back." Then I waited for the boom to be lowered.

The patrol came back around midnight, saying of course that they couldn't find the target. The next day nothing happened. Or the day after that either. In fact, I never saw or heard from the General again.

Sat'y, Sept. 9. 1944

France

Dear Baby face:

This morning I got a letter and two V-mails from you, and a letter and a V-mail from my parents. Yesterday I got one from you stamped Aug. 21 by the Post Office, but you wrote it on the 22nd, because that's the way you dated it. That's the second time that's happened. My cute little wife is so smart. She writes a letter a day after she mails it, and that's how I get the latest dope. Why don't you mail them around 10 or 11 days before you write them? Then I'll get them the same day they're written.

I just took a bath in a tub. I'm so clean I glisten. I'm completely rid of the fleas by now. That G.I. insect powder is wonderful. Since I started using it the fleas won't even talk to me.

I never lie to you, dopey. It really was a scratch. The reason I was so near a German hospital when I wrote you that letter was that we drove the Nazis right down to the sea, and when we captured the city the hospital had no place to go, so they just remained there. We've captured several hospitals that way. Anyway, by now it must be evident from my letters that I'm with my outfit. I couldn't possibly have manufactured those stories.

Sunday, Sept. 10, 1944

Dear Dopey:

We've moved quite a ways--to a new city--the biggest yet--but it's not Paris, as you would probably guess. Last night the Mayor of the city arranged a dance for the officers of my Regiment--the girls and drinks were provided free of charge--and there was plenty of both. We were all as excited as young girls going to their first dance.--It was our first dance in France--and more important still, our first since we'd been in combat. I certainly felt like a bull in a china shop --trying to dance with my hob-nailed combat shoes. I nearly broke my neck. The French dances are tricky and very different from ours. We were very self-conscious about our clothes. A lot of guys actually had blouses and pinks, but most of us just had our wool O.D.'s My pants were as baggy as a pair of sacks. I was wondering whether the Colonel would come in the same fatigues he's been wearing all over France--but no, he had on a set of O.D.'s, and was looking spry as a young chick.

I borrowed a Combat Infantryman badge from my Sergeant for the occasion--as you know, I'd sent mine home to you. It's a very impressive looking badge--the big silver rifle and silver wreath. Every girl commented on it. "How many Germans do you have to kill to get one of those?" she would ask.

"Five hundred," I answered unhesitatingly.

"Five hundred?" she repeated.

"Mai oui."

She looked at all the badges around the room. *"Mon Dieu!"* she said, making some rapid calculations. "No wonder France is free again!"

My extremely limited vocabulary presented a great problem. Even so I was much better off than most of the fellows. Even those who had several years of French in school don't seem to remember much more than *Bonjour* and *Voulez-vous*. A lot of the French girls have had some English in school, and this alleviates matters somewhat. In one way the fellows really enjoy the language obstacle. You can introduce a girl to a friend and, while the girl stands there in wide-eyed innocence, you say in a perfectly normal tone of voice, "Boy, look at those knockers --- and you should see the way she wiggles her can!" And the poor girl nods her head, smiles sweetly, and tries to summon up enough high school English to say, "Pleased to meet weeth you."

Did I ever tell you about the soldier who passed a girl on the street and said aloud, "Oh, baby, what I could do to you!"

"Well, of all the nerve!" she said, turning around and slapping him in the face. "I understood that, and I don't like it one bit!"

One of the girls gave me a little pocket dictionary and phrase book. People take speech so much for granted that they don't appreciate it. It's only when you have to struggle for five minutes to get a simple observation across that you really begin to appreciate language. This morning I found that a package arrived last night from you, and it had a German and a French dictionary. This is the first package I've received which was actually sent to my new address. However, the cocoa can was broken and everything was covered with cocoa. But I managed to brush it off all right.

Silly, your letters are not barren. They're always the most exciting thing that happens to me. Don't worry about your school work. I was flunking Physics 12 all term, and after the final I got a B. ... And if you don't feel like taking any courses during the Fall term, it's perfectly all right with me. I know that your end of the war is much harder than mine. I can remember how just after Pearl Harbor, when I was waiting for my orders, it was practically impossible for me to do any work. You're very silly to think I'd reproach you for taking the term off. ...

As they say out here about the front line troops --- you can see the enemy and the terrain --you know best what your obstacles are. I'm like the generals back in the rear who are fighting with situation maps. I can see the big picture--maybe even a little better than you--but you're much better aware of your own difficulties. You are too a brave determined woman, and I think you're very wonderful. And I love you very much. I've seen not only American girls, but English and French as well. And they've all bored me. I wish I wouldn't have to wait so long before seeing you again. I have the feeling that I may not be able to leave Europe as soon as Germany cracks, and may be stuck with some occupation assignment. The only basis for my drawing this conclusion is my linguistic attainments, such as they are. Apparently Divisions will be completely reorganized after Germany's fall, according to the published plans of the War Dep't on demobilization. And if people are picked individually instead of collectively for the job of policing, then obviously I'm a better choice than someone who speaks only English. But you know the Army--all things are possible. Besides, I don't think American troops will be used very long for policing. I think it will be turned over to the European countries. Actually anything may happen, including going to the Pacific. Don't figure on my being demobilized --- that fancy plan is only for enlisted men.

P.S.--I just saw an order awarding me the Bronze Star. They're giving those things out these days to every Joe and his brother.

***

Wed., Sept. 13, 1944

France

Dear Dopey face:

Got a letter from Rivkie yesterday dated Aug. 29. She also seems to have the idea, gathered from you via some friend of hers who visited New York, that I had my head blown off and am trying to minimize the loss. Her conclusion is strengthened by the fact that I happened to write her on Red Cross stationary, and I never even mentioned the incident (because I had forgotten it), and she assumes that I must be in a hospital too. For the benefit of all concerned, I am hale and hearty (you know I'm immortal) and will return to plague you after the war for the rest of your days. I have all my limbs, appendages, and organs in excellent working condition, and just because the Army gives medals for nothing, that's no reason to draw such conclusions.

We're near another big city, but I haven't seen it yet. Yesterday 20,000 Germans surrendered, presenting an immense problem in reverse logistics because we have to start feeding them, dammit. They'd been cut off for many days and were roaming around wondering what to do. Nobody had time to waste fooling around with them, so they were just left alone until they developed an appetite, as well as an inferiority complex. Then they sent the General a message asking if he wouldn't please attack them with, say, 2 battalions, so they could surrender. The General said he was sorry, but he was busy right now and maybe he would attack later if he had more time, but that until then they'd have to manage the best way they could. They kept getting hungrier and hungrier, and finally in desperation they offered to walk all the way over to us, if only somebody would please capture them. But it isn't easy to capture 20,000 prisoners, however anxious they may be to cooperate. So the process is still going on. But it's another Regiment of the Division that got stuck with the job. I haven't seen a Kraut in weeks.

Nothing to write about --- nothing ever happens around here anymore. I keep thinking about you all the time, day and night --- I guess it's because I've got nothing better to think about. I wish I could figure out some way to surprise you and pay you a visit, you cute little doll. Why don't you send me some pictures? Why don't I get more mail from you? Why can't I go home on leave, or something? Why can't Hitler call it a war, and stop wasting my time?

The Chaplain just came over and told me the Germans gave up all hope of surrendering to us, and had to surrender to the French, which they were afraid to do and had been trying to avoid. France, as you know, was one of the occupied countries of Europe, and the Germans aren't exactly popular with them. That's why the Nazis are always so anxious to surrender to us or the English. We're such gentlemen, you know.

Why should I write you letters when I don't get any, hardly. Now I'm going to write Rivkie and tell her all about how I got hit, which she wants to know. Love,

Your goldbricking warrior husband.

***

Wed., Sept. 13, 1944

France

Dear *(sister-in-law)* Rivkie:

The title of this letter ought to be "How I Got My Purple Heart," or "The Army gives Medals for the Damnedest Things." The reason I failed to mention my big bloody wound in my last letter was not deliberate omission, but merely that I had completely forgotten about it. I don't think it'll even leave a scar. In the Infantry scratches like that are as common as the ordinary cold is back home, and nobody pays any attention to them unless a man is killed or incapacitated, which could never happen to me, on account of I'm immortal. But since you want to know how it happened, here's the story:

It was a bad day for us, and a bloody one. Our only satisfaction was that the Germans were suffering far greater losses. Censorship requirements won't allow me to give you any percentages, but suffice it to say that our casualty rate was pretty high. We were fighting for a harbor city (no, not Brest) *(actually, St. Malo)*, and we were held up by a fortified strong point. It was quite an affair, with subterranean tunnels and all, as I learned afterwards, and it was directly in the zone of our Battalion, although the whole Division was unable to advance until it was reduced, because it dominated the terrain for miles around. The Germans were shelling us with tanks, self-propelled 88's, and mortars. I was sitting on the floor in a building which was serving as our Observation Post, and had just been admiring the structure of the building. "You know," I said to someone, "I bet this place could almost stand a direct hit." The shells were falling awfully close. The phone rang, and I picked it up to answer it. Just then came the ka-whoom! and the phone was blown out of my hand, the room crumbled and turned black, becoming so filled with dust and debris that for a few moments it was impossible to breathe. Then I realized that I was hit, because my leg was all stiffened up, and I felt that it was wet with blood. But the shrapnel fragments in my leg were very small. The big one was the one that got away. There were two nice big holes in my sleeve, one where a big chunk of shrapnel had entered, and the other where it left, missing my arm completely. Just when I was beginning to feel sorry for myself, and wondering where I could find a medic, I got word that the Colonel had been hit in the leg by a machine gun bullet, and that the S-3 had gotten one in the arm. The Colonel refused treatment, but the S-3 was being evacuated. I decided that the Colonel would be needing me, so I figured I'd just forget about the whole thing. In fact, I felt very ashamed that I had even been thinking about taking time off to be treated. When I found the Colonel things were in pretty sad shape. Our leading Company had been cut off and we couldn't even reach them by radio. Out of our three Rifle Company Commanders one was killed and one badly wounded.

His right foot had been blown off just above the ankle. When we got to him he was sitting on the ground calmly applying a tourniquet to the bloody stump. He had removed the belt from his trousers and pulled it tight above the wound to keep from bleeding to death.

Some pretty good men died that day. But, as usual in such cases, just when things looked worst for us, the Germans pulled out, and withdrew to their fortress.

On the battle for the fortress hangs another tale. We blasted them all day with heavy 4.2 inch mortars and Artillery. I lay on the floor of the attic of a house only 200 yards from the fort, together with the Artillery and mortar Forward Observers, and we pounded hell out of them. In order to get fire and observation they had to come out of their tunnels and get out on top, and that's where we really stacked them up. I never saw so many dead Germans in all my life. Talk about mass slaughter --- that was it. They ran about on the skyline to get away from our shelling. It looked just like a shooting gallery. I grabbed somebody's B.A.R. and started firing at them, and they ran around like lunatics, not knowing where to take shelter. Every time one of our 4.2 inch shells landed the whole house trembled from the concussion, and a couple of times I thought we'd get blown up ourselves. It's a good thing there were no short rounds. Then we got orders to stop firing, so a propaganda broadcast could be sent to them over the P.A. system, calling on them to surrender. We were sore as hell, because that was just when we should have attacked. By the time the broadcast was over it was dark and they hadn't surrendered, so we had to pull a night attack. But we ran into a stone wall and had to withdraw. We continued blasting them all night, and in the morning, just when we were attacking again, up came the white flag.

The Colonel sent me into the fortress to arrange the surrender. The Nazi Major was sore as hell because he had to deal with a mere 1st. Lt. It gave me a funny feeling walking inside that place with hundreds of Germans standing around and watching me. There were about 800 of them, including 200 wounded, and not counting all the dead. We didn't get along so well, this Nazi and I. He persisted in giving orders until I had to tell him to shut up --- from now on he'd be taking orders, not giving them. It was a sad day for Hitler, and there have been many like it since then.

But I'm getting away from the original story --- about the Purple Heart. The Colonel and I went hobbling around on our one good leg apiece --- jumping over fences like a couple of 4 F's. Then when evening came he went to the Battalion Aid station to get repaired, and I went along, not because my wound was severe enough to warrant it, but because the leg was beginning to swell up, and I was afraid of infection. The medics picked out the splinters and taped it up. It stopped hurting right there, and I was ready to go back to work. It was a very minor incident in a very eventful battle, and that was why I never mentioned it to you in my letter, not because I was trying to hide it.

Since then we've fought our way through a couple of cities, and took one island, but for the most part things have been pretty quiet, and I've been living rather comfortably. In the last couple of weeks I haven't done a goddamned thing, and I'm about bored to death. I wish Hitler would call the whole thing off so I could get back to something interesting, like my engineering, not to mention my dopey wife.

You're lucky to be taking interesting courses and looking like Ingrid B., and you always were a nice zaftig babe (God bless you --- you certainly would go over big out here).

Right now the Colonel is lying on the floor on top of my sleeping bag, and every time somebody comes in he yells, "Quiet! You'll wake up the flies."

Love and kisses from your soldiering b.i.l.

P.S. You going to Hawaii? How will I get to see you when I come home if you're in Hawaii?

***

Thur., Sept. 14, 1944

France

Dear Dopey funny face you:

Got your letter of Aug. 31 yesterday. Also a V-mail from Nat Eisenstadt in England. Couldn't for the life of me remember who the hell he was at first. His letter is very funny --- it was addressed to my old Replacement Battalion address. "What do your activities consist of?" he writes. "Right now I'm listening to a broadcast on the war front." Then he tells me all about how our troops are doing so well in France. "For recreation," he says, "I go to town to take in a movie, go to the Red Cross Club ... . Nothing very exciting, as you yourself have undoubtedly experienced." Apparently he hasn't been informed of the nature of my recreational activities.

You're awful cute when you try to guess where I am, especially when after playing around with several coastal cities you say, "Maybe you're not even there. Maybe you're in St. Malo or someplace like that." Why did St. Malo seem so impossible? Anyway, we've moved several times since that.

147

I dreamed about you too last night --- all night --- and I think it was the first time since I arrived in France that I dreamed at all. A lot of the others have battle nightmares, but I always sleep a quiet dreamless sleep. But I've always thought about you in the daytime. I daydream all the time. Now of course I'm developing lazy habits, since I have nothing to do. I went to town last night --- one of the biggest cities in France --- but I like the last one we were at much better. Don't know how I'll even manage if I ever get into combat again. Long rests are demoralizing.

There's a big German underground network of caves near here, full of liquors, wines, and food --- enough to feed a Division for months. Everybody's been helping himself, and they've overeaten so much that today they all have the G.I.'s. Except me. I went swimming yesterday in a nice little lake near here. It's funny how I've gotten used to going swimming in the nude even when women are around. It doesn't embarrass me at all. In France there is nothing like the complicated frustration mores we have back home. People are extremely frank about all such things. A man will urinate off the side of the road, and when a lady comes by he doesn't stop --- just tips his hat and says *Bonjour*. In the parks the urinals are practically right out in the open.

Wish I'd get more up-to-date news from you. There are all kinds of rumors around about how far inside Germany Patton's troops are.

The Germans have shattered a whole generation or more in Europe. The French people have been reduced to a horrible level. You can see just what it means for a country to be under Fascist domination. Children have no childhood, women are forced to turn to prostitution to survive, the men are killed or forced to work for the Nazis. These people burn with such hatred for the Germans that they would gladly see the whole nation completely annihilated. The stories of what went on before we came are unbelievable. After all, France, unlike Russia, was conquered. But mass murder was practiced here too. A girl we met in a cafe in town last night started bawling like a baby when she told us what had happened. A German soldier was killed by the underground, and the Germans started a mass slaughter of French civilians. They dragged 8 - month infants out of their cradles and killed them together with their mothers. To Americans these stories are like from another world. Back home of course they were labelled by our worldly-wise people as "war propaganda," but here our soldiers are stunned by what they see and hear. It's all so hard to associate these acts with the sniveling prisoners who whine about international law and the Geneva convention. No wonder they're so afraid of being captured by the French. One of the things that made the island fortress surrender to us was that the Commander was informed that if he held out any longer the Americans would have to leave, and the handling of the matter would be turned over to French forces.

I look at the Germans, and try to figure out why they do the things they do. Sometimes when there's plenty of time I even ask them, and try to get the psychology behind it. It's really not so hard to understand. When a conqueror defeats an Army, and all is quiet again, he can afford to be gentlemanly. But when a whole people is being reduced to slavery, and tries to fight back, what else is there to do but kill women and babies? There's no other way for the Nazis to fight back. No wonder they invent flying bombs --- it's the only air weapon left them. And when a German soldier is stabbed in the back, how else can they fight back but with terror? These results flow inevitably from the original source of Fascism and slavery. You can't be a successful Nazi and kill only soldiers. You have to kill everyone.

That's what I try to tell our soldiers when they talk about wiping out the German nation. It can happen to any nation. All that's necessary is for the Fascists to get in power. They'd raise a generation of animals back in the States just as easily as the Nazis did in Germany. I can even pick out some individuals who would make excellent candidates.

It's pathetic what's happened here, especially to the women, and the children talk like adults. Nothing has been kept from them. They've seen it all --- rape, murder, brutality. A whole continent seems to have been twisted out of shape here by the Nazi scourge.

I'm enclosing a reprint from Stars & Stripes on the 83rd. The reason the Division was on the secret list for such a long time was that German intelligence reports had us completely wiped out, and it was preferable to disillusion them the hard way.

149

The Germans weren't so far off the mark. I had seen our Regimental casualty figures, and they were well over 100% per month in Normandy. Nor could it have been very different in the battle for St. Malo. We were the same Division, but not the same individuals.

***

Thur., Sept. 14, 1944

1900 hours

France

Dear Dopey-who-has-to-sleep-under-horses:

I wrote you a letter this morning, but on account of you're such a sweet baby and sent me two letters today, I'm going to write you another. One of your letters is dated Sept. 1, and the other Sept. 6, from that horse place you're at. And I hope you stay there, because that letter took only 8 days to get here--must have come by pony express. Are you having a nice time, and I hope if you sleep under the horses you brought an umbrella.

As a further reward to you for being such a good girl I'm making up a package tonight to send you. It will include (a) one pair of earrings I bought some time ago but never got around to mailing, (b) the firing mechanism on one of the booby traps that came off Dopey Dora Island, and (c) some A. Hitler candy for you to chew on. I wish I could send you all the wonderful A. Hitler candy and cookies and chicken noodle soup and roast beef and *vin blanc* and *vin rouge* and rum and champagne and fruit and wurst and ice cream mix and all the other numerous and unlimited supplies of food and drink out of which we manage to eke out a bare existence. However, if they're starving you at that horse place, just let me know what you need and I'll send it to you. I can't send you everything we have because there's no room in the Atlantic Ocean for all that stuff, but I'll do the best I can.

Aaaah! the Colonel just gave me a shot of A. Hitler brandy. Vile stuff, but I manage to force it down.

Don't worry about losing my Combat Infantryman badge. I swiped me a new one today, because they look so pretty and I haven't had one to wear, and I started this rumor about how it means you killed 500 Nazis.

I'm glad we're saving so much money, but it seems wasteful to spend it on horses, when there are so many good A. Hitler horses around here. Wish I could send one home.

Please let me know if you need anything. I know things are very scarce in the States, with rationing and all. And let me know if packages arrive in good condition.

Somebody finally got a cable around here today--the Executive Officer. "Darling," it said. "Let us know if you were hurt badly. Please tell the truth. Don't keep anything from us. Love." It was signed by someone he had never heard of, and moreover, he's never been wounded. I think maybe you should stop sending me cables. They probably arrive somewhere in China, addressed to Chiang-kai-Shek.

Sure send me a package with lots of stuff to eat. A. Hitler will probably run out of stuff eventually if he keeps on feeding the A.E.F.

Give my love to Ma Yokum and all the horses and Sherry and everybody. I bet I know where you're hurting right now, you cute thing you. If it gets very rough you can put in for a transfer from Cavalry to Infantry. But don't say I didn't warn you.

So long, you long-legged little cowboy. Oh, what I could do to you.

Your foot slogging Infantry husband.

P.S. - How much are they paying you to stay at that horse place?

P.S.S. - Shall I send you some stationery?

***

Sat'y, Sept. 16, 1944

France

Dear Cowgirl:

I don't particularly feel in a writing mood (I'm so bored), but you've been such a good girl, and I got three letters from you in today's and yesterday's mail, and I'm getting 8 days service on a lot of letters, that I ought to do something about it. So I'll tell you how I spent the last couple of days of my vacation.

Day before yesterday a rather well-dressed young Frenchman rode into our area on a bicycle, and in impeccable English said that his family would be greatly honored if some of our officers were to have dinner with him and his family some evening at their home. He had a couple of not at all bad looking babes with him, so everybody said, "But yes." We went last night, and it turned out to be at a beautiful castle built in the 16th century and called *Chateau de Paty*. It had a drawbridge and a moat, and the stream could be used for fishing and swimming. To catch a fish all you had to do was throw a line into the water and pull it out --- there would be a fish on the hook every time. They gave us picture postcards of the place, but I can't send you one, because postcards are barred from the mails (they reveal your location). The head of the house was a Paris surgeon, and it was a large and apparently rather wealthy family --- the house was full of servants, the food and drink was of the very best, the grounds were beautiful and well-kept, as were the five daughters. For us it was an evening well spent --- much better than the crazy wild evenings the fellows like to spend in town. I learned a hell of a lot of French. If I could spend a lot of time that way I would really learn the language. These people were well educated and fairly intelligent, in spite of being wealthy. They were very nice, and full of hatred for the Nazis and Petain, and we drank many toasts to *Vive l' Amerique* and *Vive la France.* "It was very nice of you to invite us," we said. "We have been waiting for you," they replied. "Four years is a long time." French is the easiest language I've ever encountered. Do you realize that I've been living in France for three months now?

Yesterday afternoon was spent on a crazy expedition. A call came from Regiment that there were two German officers holding out in the cellar of a house, and refusing to surrender, so I went to flush them out. "How many men will you need?" said the Colonel.

"Two or three," I said.

"Take six," he said. "And get a bazooka --- and take plenty of hand grenades. And be careful. Use your grenades."

"Maybe they've got Lugers," I said. "You want a Luger, Colonel?"

"Listen," said Schmitt. "I want a pair of boots. But let's have no unnecessary bloodshed. Ask them if they wear 10 1/2 C before you shoot them."

So I started out with two jeeps, looking like a rolling arsenal, bristling with tommy guns, grenades, bazooka, rifles, and pistols. I felt silly riding around like that way back here, and I knew it would be a false alarm. These civilian reports always are. We went to FFI headquarters-- they were supposed to know where it was. They gave me a guide who led me to another guide who led me to another guide who led me to another guide, who said he would take me to somebody who knew where it was. Before long you couldn't see the jeeps for all the people riding all over the hoods and hanging on the sides. "Now tell me what it's all about," I asked the "Man Who was Supposed to Know."

"I'll take you to the house where the Russians are," he said.

"Russians?" I asked. "What Russians?" What trick of fate is always involving me with Russians?

The upshot of it was that nobody knew anything about it, except that one man had seen two civilians enter this house two days previously, and claimed he could recognize them from 1940 as German officers. On the strength of that, as I learned subsequently, several FFI bureaucrats had entered the house and beaten up the Russian. The latter claimed he had never seen any Germans. He lived at the house with his family. There were obviously no Germans in the house, and probably never had been.

The other day we got a report that there were 150 Germans holding out in the woods somewheres. Investigation revealed that there were only 100, then 50, then 25, then three, and finally, when the origin of the report was tracked down, it was learned that somebody had heard two shots fired the day before, and that's all it was.

Many a time on combat reconnaissance I've been diverted by reports of "snipers," which invariably turned out to be some G.I.'s firing into the bushes at their own imagination.

Wow, I'm sleepy. Everybody's gone into town to raise some hell.

Sunday, Sept. 17, 1944

Dear Dopey:

Since I painted your name all over my jeep, whenever I ride down the street, people yell, "Hey, dopey!" and it makes me feel like I'm home again.

I'm trying to answer four of your letters at once, as well as one of Sherry's.

I think you might as well stop buying Collier's. I don't believe there'll ever be a story about my outfit. That phoney correspondent Henry C. Gorell just took a few officers for a ride, pumped them for information and liquor, and made all kinds of promises which he never intended to keep. He came to St. Malo weeks after the fighting was over, and probably wrote about it as if he were there at the time. Any time you see his by-line on a U.P. story, you can spot it as a tissue of lies. Right now I'm looking at Stars and Stripes, which has a piece by him headlined, "With a U.S. Armored Column Inside Germany." He says he witnessed the penetration of the Siegfried line, "Standing within rifle shot of the much-propagandized German fortifications." You can be pretty sure that if he was within rifle shot, there was no one shooting the rifles. You'd be surprised how obviously phony these stories are, and how evident it is that the correspondent never got there till long after the action was over. I could quote a lot of statements in his story to show you how ridiculous these correspondents are, but why waste any more of my time or yours.

It's funny that Stars and Stripes has carried nothing about the *Vernichtungslager* in Lublin. Most of us here wouldn't have too much trouble believing the stories, especially if we've talked to the French at all, but I imagine back home there is still a lot of this "war propaganda" cynicism. I don't think I ever told you about the German wallet we found with a photograph of seven or eight civilians, including some women and young boys and girls, hanging from a gallows. The clothing and background suggested that it had been taken in Russia or Poland. Together with this snapshot were pictures of the man's wife and children. It's a lucky thing for the Nazi who threw this wallet away at the last minute that it wasn't found on his person, or there would have been one less prisoner and one more stinking Heinie corpse for the Graves Registration people to handle.

The newspapers all made a big fuss about the Citadel, and said little about St. Joseph *Festung*. Actually the latter dominated the approaches to the city, while the former was out on a peninsula and was reduced at leisure after the city was taken. But when it was safe in St. Malo and the correspondents could walk around with safety, the Citadel was out of ammunition for its big guns. In the earlier days, when one of these big guns was killing our men, and we were still mopping up in the city (there were no correspondents there that I know of), a couple of my boys, using a captured German BC scope we got at St. Joseph, spotted the muzzle flash. That BC scope is a beautiful instrument, and I've adopted it as an organic piece of equipment. We got the gun right under the cross-hairs of the scope, and you could see it fire, and then wait for about seven seconds until the round landed only around 200 yards away from where we were. It was funny --- you look at the harmless little flash, and then wait for the shell to come. Every time one dropped, the whole building we were in shook as though it would fall apart. It was pretty heavy stuff. I took a compass reading on the gun, timed the interval between the flash and the sound, and phoned the coordinates of the gun position back to our Cannon Company Commander, Brown. Then the fun began. The

Colonel and the Executive Officer came running over to get in on the fire adjustment.

The first round splashed in the water to the right. "Two hundred right. One hundred over," I said into the phone.

It took about two minutes before we were registered on the target. "Twenty-five left," I said. "Repeat range. Fire for effect."

"On the way," said Brownie. Then, soon after, as we were watching breathlessly, "Battery has fired." Now it was a matter of seconds.

When the rounds landed it looked good. You could see bodies blown into the air, and then come floating down again.

"How we doing?" said Brownie.

"Wonderful," I told him. "You can hear them screaming."

"Like a repeat performance?" he asked.

"How's the ammunition situation?"

"Listen," he said. "Is it doing any good?"

"Sure it's doing good," I told him. "It's killing Heinies, isn't it?"

"O.K.," he said. "Repeat fire for effect. Right?"

"Right," I said.

And then we did it again and again. But the gun had stopped firing, and the crew had taken cover. I doubt if that's the firing you saw in the newsreels. It was too early. But it was the same place. I got a picture of it later just after the surrender, with the Stars and Stripes waving in the breeze.

In the year 2001, the 84-year old reincarnation of the 26-year old who wrote this letter in 1944 is finding it hard to identify with the writer of that time. The hatred engendered by all the killing and dying had left its mark. I have no memory of actually seeing bodies blown into the air, but I distinctly remember yelling that I could practically hear them screaming.

I would answer Sherry's nice letter all about how you made a big hit with the horses and men in your red bathing suit, but I don't know her address. She has a somewhat illegible scrawl like Carl, and writes like radio programs and short stories and things. Give her a hug for me. I suppose Carl is home by this time. I wish I could see you in that bathing suit.

Your horse Diamonds sounds like he has an interesting personality. So does the J. Cagney character who owns the ranch. Only if he's so tough, why doesn't he come out here? There have been a couple of times when we could have used J. Cagney and P. O'Brien if they'd been around. To tell you the truth, there is very little relationship between Hollywood toughness and the combat variety. When the shells come whooping over it cuts them all down to the same size. Some Sergeants who were the terrors of their outfits back in the States have turned out to be the meekest under fire. You never see these guys till the battle is over. And other men who have always been very quiet sometimes turn out to be the best. You can't generalize though. There's no way of telling in advance. We have one 1st Sergeant who talks tough and fights the same way. He usually scares the Germans to death. Every time he sees some prisoners he says, "Well, I'll be damned. How'd I ever overlook them?" Once he saw a prisoner whose looks he didn't like. He grabbed a rifle with a bayonet on it, emptied the ammunition, and tossed it over to the German. He then picked up another rifle and bayonet and brought it to the ready position. The German looked at the rifle, looked at the Sergeant, and then tossed the rifle down and put his hands up again.

I have no memory of either the Sergeant or the episode, which was hardly inspirational.

That particular Sergeant is a great showman, but can fight besides. They're not all like that. You can never tell till the situation arises.

I'm glad you're having such a good time, baby. You'll be such a good rider that you'll put me to shame.

157

***

Sunday nite, Sept. 17, 1944

France

Dear Dopey:

Everything comes to him wot waits. How true, how true. Today nobody got any mail but me. All I got was 24 letters from you, 11 from my parents, one from Mark Reich in Italy (April 11), and one from the Ft. Meade Officers Club, asking me to give them two bucks for services rendered during the month of May, which I spent at sea and in England. Boy, will I write them a sarcastic letter. There were also two cablegrams from my silly wife, dated July 28 and Aug. 11. The amusing thing about them was the caption on the back of the envelopes --- "THE FAST ROUTE."

I had intended to go out for the evening, but I had a much better time staying in and reading your dopey letters. In fact, it was the best time I've had in a long time. Never had so much fun since we blew up that big gun in the Citadel. I learned several things, including how you got an A in Chemistry by vamping your prof. From the dates on these things they must have been routed through Vladivostok.

"Ha, ha, ha," says the Colonel, reading the newspapers. "That screwy phony pacifist, Oswald Garrison Villard."

"Is he still sounding off?" I ask.

"You know what he did?" says the Colonel. "Fainted on the altar on his wedding day. Ho, ho, ho!"

Schmitt is reading the papers too. "Tell me," he says. "Of what strategic importance is the Italian front?"

"Why, it's strategically important, that's what it is," says the Colonel.

"I don't see how," says Schmitt.

"Well, get on the ball then, dammit," says the Colonel.

I am eating fudge and drinking a bottle of red wine they gave us at the Chateau. They make their own wine there. This section of France is a great wine-producing region.

"Burn all secret documents!" says the Colonel. "We're surrounded. Germans to the right of us, Germans to the left of us." He watches me as I go scratching away with my pen. "What in hell do you write about? Scribble, scribble, scribble. Someday I'm gonna make you read it to me, so I can hear all that crap you're turning out."

How can I answer so many letters, except you write me such wonderful letters, and you're so wonderful, and I'm so lucky to have such a wife, and all I want is you, and there are no other babes who can hold a candle to you.

Went swimming today. Probably the last time. Getting too cool. War better end right away. Getting too cold. Won't be fun any more.

***

Wed., Sept. 20, 1944

France

Dear Dopey Dora:

I am so bored and tired of this life. I went to another wealthy chateau last night for an extremely delicious and sumptuous chicken dinner. Our Battalion has gotten involved with this wealthy family from Martinique, and we keep getting dinner invitations. It's all very nice seeing how the other half lives --- very amusing. We were discussing French authors, and somewhere Andre Gide came under discussion. "I don't like his politics," I said. "Oh, but he's changed," they said. "His politics is all right now!" They're very nice people. They keep making you feel as though you're doing them a tremendous favor eating all their food and being entertained. They feel that they've been freed from slavery and there's nothing too good for the Americans who did it.

I've been in a very bad mood lately --- I've become very irritated with everything and everybody. Yesterday I had to stand in a formation for nearly two hours while the General awarded all the Bronze Stars, and hear all the lengthy orders read, and the General's perorations. It was very silly. For them it's still a football game --- we did it for the glory of the Division, according to the General, and we must see to it that the Division keeps the best reputation in the Army. He actually thinks we lived with Death all those weeks just to give his Division a good reputation. Why are there always more horse's asses than there are horses?

Right now there is a German program on the radio. The closer we get to Germany, the more clearly their stations come across. They are playing very pretty music. It's funny, how for all my violent hatred for the Nazis I still have such a warm feeling for the German language and music, and even for the people. The closer I get to the country, the stronger this feeling grows. I get this feeling for every new country I come to. Now I'm all excited and anxious to get there. I know the German people must be held in account for all that Nazism has done, and yet down deep inside I keep apologizing for the people, and telling myself that what the Nazis have done has nothing to do with the *deutsche Gemütlichkeit und Seele.* It could have happened anywheres. I have seen so many Germans die that I have almost come to identify the nation with the rather unpleasant state. But at the same time I've talked with hundreds of Germans, and seen countless diaries and letters and snapshots, and there is a distinct difference between the Nazi ideology and the ordinary German nature, which is no different from that of any other country. Given 10 or 11 years, any nation can be turned into a nation of beasts if the political gangsters gain power. My comrades-in-arms don't share my opinions, and the French certainly don't. They hate the whole German nation. But it's pretty hard for me to hate any nation. All the fellows talk about how they'll really run rampant when they reach Germany, and frankly, there's very little difference between the things they speak of doing and the things the Germans did in the occupied countries. The big difference between us and them is that our Army will not tolerate such things, while the German Army encouraged them. All that is necessary is for gangsterism to be legalized, and there will always be plenty of candidates. And the honest people just get snowed under, --- because decency is more of a negative trait --- a matter of not hurting others, --- while Fascism is so positive. Of course as you know, honesty can be put on a positive basis, but unfortunately the group of people who have learned how are still very much in the minority.

You know what I mean? Or do you think I'm a soft-hearted dope? I don't think so --- I mean about being soft-hearted, although maybe I'm a dope. I have been very cruel when I felt that cruelty furthered the accomplishment of our mission. But I can't bring myself to hate a people --- worse yet, I can't even get myself to stop liking them. And I hope our soldiers will be curbed inside Germany. I don't believe that the cause of freedom will be advanced by permitting the mistreating of a civilian population. I'm quite sure our Army won't permit such things.

But you'd be surprised how much alike all peoples are, no matter what language they speak --- even the Germans aren't so different from the rest of us. There but for the grace of God go I. What do you think? Have I been in a rest area so long that I'm going softie?

I'm sleepy as hell. Been going out too much. Going to bed early tonight.

We've just started a discussion of French politics --- that irresistible muddle.

So long, sweetheart darling.

***

Friday, Sept. 22, 1944

France

Dear Dopey:

The restriction on sending postcards has been lifted, so I'm sending you one of the Chateau I visited a couple of times --- in fact, I was there only last night. The people are very nice, and I have their Paris address, in case I'm ever there. I've had dinner at several such Chateaus --- there

161

doesn't seem to be anything the French people --- both rich and poor --- won't do for the Americans.

I can also tell you of places I've visited --- a couple of evenings ago I was at Tours. Angers is the nicest town I've seen yet. That was where the Mayor arranged a dance for my Regiment. You know by now from the clipping I sent you of the places we fought at --- near Carentan, the St. Lo-Perier highway, Dol, Chateauneuf, St. Malo-Parame-St. Servan, Dinard, Isle de Cezembre (surrendered at the last minute).

I've been eating too many dinners --- got a bellyache.

I'm sending you the complete order on my Bronze Star through the Base censor --- although it's classified Confidential. Wotta lotta baloney those decorations. In the Field Artillery you become a hero every time you go as far forward as Regimental CP, while in a Rifle Company in the Infantry you risk your life every two minutes and it's just an everyday occurrence. It's the most inequitable thing I ever heard of. As usual the doughboy gets the worst end of the deal. But after all, what's the difference. They can cheapen the medals, but they can't cheapen what the war is all about, although they try hard enough.

There is a very nasty regulation which forbids our writing any information to the families of our friends who are killed or missing. They write letters that tear your heart out, begging for any details about how the man was killed, what he did in the last few minutes, etc., etc. And we can't tell them a thing. There was one officer who led a combat patrol I sent out which was practically wiped out. I was only 150 yards away when it happened, and we found the bodies of a couple of them, while the others were missing. Later, when we captured a German Battalion C.P., we found the officer's papers, and I have very good reason to believe that he was taken prisoner. We got a letter from his wife today begging for information --- and I can't tell her a thing. All that's allowed is for the Chaplain to write the usual condolences. Of course there's a reason for this regulation, but sometimes it seems very stupid. It can bring such a great deal of comfort to the families to give them this information. You should see those letters. As far I'm concerned, I wouldn't mind war so much if it weren't for such things.

Gee, dopey, but I'd like to get some mail. How was your vacation, good? Why don't you write me? The Chaplain took my picture today. Maybe he'll get it developed someday and I'll be able to send it to you. Every time somebody takes pictures and tries to get them developed, we move out before we can pick them up.

Everybody has started talking about the usual topic --- battle experiences, close shaves --- "I'll never forget the day when ... , etc., etc."

So long, funny face. Remember me? I'm your husband.

***

At night Sat'y, Sept. 23, 1944

France

Dear Dopey darling:

I miss you very much tonite. I just got your letter of Sept. 11 from that horse place, and it's the first one in a long time. The mail situation has been bad, and I think it will become worse. I just got one from Al Crane, who in his letter performs a remarkable feat of geographical guesswork. He tells me that in my region of France people speak the very best language. He even speaks of the Renaissance Chateaus, one of which is on the post card I sent you.

I'm tired of always writing letters. It'll be over soon, I think. As soon as we've made the necessary adjustments to the lengthened supply lines, we'll whoosh right through. Wish us luck.

That Brest deal we missed was quite a scrap. Bloody as they come. Sometimes those goddam Nazis make me so sore I want to see every last German killed. I'm getting sick and tired of them and their god damned stupid stubbornness.

Wait around for me. I'll be back one of these days. Give yourself a big hug and a kiss.

P.S. -- I feel good. How do you feel? Huh? Hello.

ADOLPH BAKER

***

9 LUXEMBOURG

We had left the Loire valley and moved east to Luxembourg, but I was not allowed to say so in the first letters. We were now part of the Third Army. The idea was to set up a defense line at the Moselle River, which separated Luxembourg from Germany. My Battalion started out being in reserve, and it was the softest duty we had ever had.

Tuesday, Sept. 26, 1944

Somewhere in Europe

Dear Dopey:

Everybody is sitting around a fire chewing the fat, arguing everything from why do the Germans keep on fighting to why don't we have 4.2 mortars in an Infantry Regiment. We're now located in a hunting lodge which would be very nice if the plumbing hadn't been wrecked by a few silly rifle bullets. However, we're fixing that up. Now they're arguing Roosevelt and Dewey, who's better.

You can't imagine all the interesting things I've seen in the last few days. There's no language barrier for me here, and I have a helluva good time talking to the people. They hate the Germans even worse than the French do. All the young men have been sent by the Germans to fight on the Russian front. "You know what they ought to do with the best

German there is?" a guerrilla fighter said to me. "--- Hang him from the highest tree in this forest." I have never seen so many children as there are here. This is a country of children. And when you go by in a jeep they all come out and start shouting at the tops of their lungs. This is some of the most beautiful country I've seen yet, and the beer here is a joy to all mankind.

Now they're talking about ice cream. Colonel says he likes a hot fudge sundae. Everybody is describing all the gooey ice cream combinations they go for. Now they're telling dirty jokes. How do they get from one subject to another this way? Send me some clippings or something quoting the dopey things Dewey says, so I can expose him properly.

I can't write with everybody shootin' the bull around here. I'm going to bed. G'nite, sleepy dopey.

***

2200, Friday, Sept. 29, 1944

Europe

Dear Dopey:

It's a beautiful moon out --- I bet you can see it too when it gets around to your side. We just sat out on the ground and saw a Hollywood movie --- "Two Girls and a Sailor." It was a swell picture, full of girls' bosoms and legs ---real pretty girls --- the kind of movie our boys like best to see. --- It's such a pleasant contrast to the war. It's funny. Only a short distance from here is the enemy, and yet we can sit out in the open without even a slit trench, and look at a nice warm movie that takes us all the way home. The Nazis can't do this. For them the dying and the screaming for medics never stops. This is as it should be.

I had a nightmare last night. I dreamed you didn't love me anymore, and it was like the old days when you used to cause me so many heartaches. You do love me, don't you, dopey darling? It must be nearly a week since I heard from you. It's very hard to wait for mail that never comes, and it's very hard to write when I don't hear from you.

Yesterday I drove over to a town that had just been liberated. The people were out in the streets celebrating. They were dividing up the wine stocks of the *Bürgermeister* --- he had been one of the collaborators, and left with his Nazi pals. They offered me some of the wine, and it was really very good. Just before our troops entered the town the people rounded up the remaining German soldiers and made them sweep up all the streets. "Have some plums," an old man said to me, showing me a basket. "Have some more plums."

Schmitt just coined a great one. He said, "Eat, drink, and be merry, for tomorrow you have dysentery." There's been quite a bit of stomach trouble --- maybe from drinking too much beer. Hasn't bothered me though.

This is a very unusual country. Most of the people know several languages. Even the little children are linguists. Quite a few people speak English. It's very surprising at times. I was driving the Company Commanders around on a reconnaissance, when we passed the cutest brunette we've seen since we came to this country. "You'd better ask the way," said one of the officers.

"Pardon me," I said to the girl in German. "But which way is the town of --- ?

"You're going the wrong way," she answered in perfect English, with hardly the trace of an accent.

"You speak very good English," I said.

"It is very kind of you to say so."

"No," I said. "It's the truth. Where did you learn English?"

"In school," she replied. It turned out she had had only three years of English in school, and had never even been to England. It's really remarkable the knack these people have for languages.

"You speak better English," I said, "than anyone else I've met here."

"Oh," she gave me a big bright smile. "You know how to flatter." Then, as an afterthought, "Where did you learn to speak such good German?"

"In der Schule," I said. The boys all crowded around, and we wasted around twenty minutes kidding around with her. We departed unwillingly. In my business there's no time for long acquaintances.

Don't try to guess where I am, dopey. You'll be dead wrong, I assure you. This is really beautiful country. Great big rolling fields. There are no farmhouses. Instead people gather in little villages, and only go to their farms when they want to work the land.

It was a pretty tough break the boys got who landed at Arnhem. I guess we can't always have good news. You think it'll be awfully long now, baby? I'm really very tired of the war. I feel like it ought to be over by now. I know the dangers of dizziness from success, but I can't help it. I'm awfully homesick for you. And war is a pretty unpleasant racket.

So long, beautiful. Don't leave me in my dreams any more.

P.S. I'm not where you think I am.

Censorship regulations are so contradictory. First they said we couldn't mention Belgium, or Holland, or Germany, or Luxembourg, etc. Now a directive just arrived saying we can mention having visited towns 25 or more miles from our location. So I am hereby informing you that I have visited the city of Esch, in the Grand Duchy of Luxembourg.

For the benefit of any censor who decides to object to that, --- why do they put out circulars like Circular No. 54, Hq., 3rd Army? That's my authority.

So long, pieface.

***

Sunday, Oct. 1, 1944

Europe

Dear Dopey:

It's a dull rainy Sunday. I slept through breakfast, got up late, and am just killing the day. The men have been authorized six-hour passes to the city of ----- . It's too nasty out to go anywhere.

I accomplished two big things yesterday --- I voted and I took a bath. The bath was a much bigger accomplishment. I'm ashamed to tell you when I took my last one. It's too cold for swimming, even if there were any lakes around here. The last time I took a complete bath was when I went swimming. Winter is a hard time to keep clean. Anyway, there is a public shower establishment in town, and I took a nice long hot shower. It was the first shower since I left England.

Did I tell you I heard from Mark Reich a couple of times. It's funny how everybody thinks he's in such grave danger regardless of how far behind the lines he is. Actually back at Division there isn't the slightest indication that there's a war going on. When I was back at a Replacement Bn. in France, and I heard our Artillery booming, I actually used to clap my helmet on my head. In those days I hadn't learned how to distinguish outgoing mail from incoming. I guess everything's relative.

Anyway, we had a lecture on Photo-interpretation scheduled one day, and the Company Commanders and I went to hear the lecture. It was given by the Division Photo-interpreter. He was a typical Ritchie boy --- loud-mouthed, blown up with a sense of self-importance. Absolutely devoid of the least trace of modesty. I wonder if I will find civilians as irritating after the war as I find some of these rear echelon people now. The lecture consisted of a peroration on the hard lot of the photo-interpreter. "There are actually nights," he said, "when I've gone with only two or two and a half hours sleep. You probably don't believe that, do you?" The officers sitting there had fought with the Infantry all the way through Normandy and Brittany, but they didn't bat an eye or crack a smile. I sure am glad I got out of that phony PI racket when I did. They sure do have a racket though. Get to go back to London periodically and rest up from nothing.

This is wonderful country for tanks and observed Artillery fire. The front line units report that the Germans are always pulling some silly stunts that get them blown off the map. Some jackass of a Nazi officer rides up in a car, and everybody heils Hitler, and they hold a big meeting and march over to some house for a big pow-wow --- all under the observation of our Artillery O.P.'s 5,000 or 6,000 yards away. As soon as they get a big crowd in the building for their meeting, a couple of Battalions of our Artillery lay in on the building, which as often as not turns out to be one of our concentration points. And that's the end of the building, meeting, Nazis, and all. What a difference from the old hedgerows of Normandy, where you couldn't see more than 150 or 200 yards in front of you. The type of soldiers our people are running into now are somewhat different from the ones back there. These are a lot of Hitler *Jugend* brats and OCS students. They are fanatical Nazis, but damn fools. They do very stupid things like the above, and pull crazy attacks that get them all wiped out. But they fight rough when they get up close. They don't have enough sense to surrender when their situation is hopeless, so they get themselves killed. Maybe it's just as well. They are like a bunch of young animals. I'm not talking from personal experience, however, only from hearsay, since we're not up on the line, and are still on vacation. So anything I tell you may be no more authentic than the newspaper reports, which isn't saying very much.

God damn it!

The mail orderly just came in, and not a goddam thing for me. Are you writing or not? I'm so disgusted, I don't even feel like writing any more letters home. What's the use? I never get any answers. Those goddam button boys are screwing up again. They're probably dumping all my mail in the ocean, or something. The bastards. I'm tired of the war anyway. I won't fire a shot until I get some mail. I just won't fight, that's all. The hell with them.

So long, you little stinker.

P.S. Please write me some letters.

***

Tuesday, Oct. 3, 1944

Europe

Dear Dopey face:

The mail finally broke through. Yesterday I got a measly little old card from your horse place dated around two years ago, but today I got three letters from you, and two from my mother. Two of yours were dated Sept. 19, and one Sept. 25. There is a tremendous gap of letters which have never arrived, however. I see that you haven't heard from me either for around 18 days.

As usual when some of your letters are held up, you casually ring in some new names on me as if they were life-long friends. Who is this Danny character, and what does he want? Why isn't he in the Army, and if he's too essential for that, then surely he can find a better use for his time than chasing a soldier's wife. I try not to be resentful toward civilians, but let me tell you right now --- that dodo better not be hanging around when I come home, or he'll wish he was in Syracuse. Sure I'm jealous. I want you to go out and have fun, but I don't think I like this particular character. Believe me, dopey, I'd like to take some of these slick essential-job bohemians up to the front lines so they might learn to have a little respect for combat soldiers. I was up there this afternoon on a reconnaissance, and I realized how much I had forgotten it all --- the whoom-whoom of incoming mail, and the faces of men who had just returned from a combat patrol that had been shot up. I'm not mad at you or anything, but I just don't like this guy. If I'm wrong correct me. But I'm really very jealous of you, dopey. I hardly ever think of anything else, and I don't like having these 4-F essentials operating where I can't get my hands on them. From over here it doesn't look as amusing to see guys chasing you as it did when I was back home. War makes people a little sensitive, that's all. Also, I'm kind of fond of you.

As for all that other stuff about volunteering for the Pacific or the front lines, or the Army of Occupation --- well, in the first place, as I've often told you, you overestimate me greatly. You actually think I'm a big hero, or something, and that I like to be up where men are dying. Actually, it takes a political discussion with myself to get my head out of a hole when things are kind of hot --- and besides I never volunteer for anything --- that's why I'm no hero. There are too many conflicts --- you are one of the biggest. I honestly wouldn't be afraid to die if it weren't for you and my parents. I don't intend to volunteer for service in the Pacific, or any other service, as a matter of fact. It's not like when I was at Grand Central Palace. I'm not a fresh case any more, and the Army is certainly not spoiling me. I've been through some of the bloodiest fighting of this war, and it's enough to satisfy any conscience. I wouldn't mind being stationed near you for a while (to tell the truth, I'd kind of like it). Everybody bitches about the idea of going to the Pacific after this is over. The only way I differ is that I won't bitch. If that's where they send me, then that's where I'll go --- without a peep. I know it's necessary for somebody to fight there, and it's easy to say let them get somebody who hasn't done any fighting, but things just don't work that way. Actually, however, I don't think that so many troops will have to be sent to the Far East from here. It's more likely that I'll be stuck with some occupation duty, in view of my knowledge of German, which is becoming quite fluent as a result of the practice I've had. Of course you know how unpredictable the Army is though.

As for volunteering for the front lines, well --- as you've probably gathered, that isn't going to be necessary. The rumor I passed on to you about how we were going to be "saved" for Occupation forces was a good rumor, and I knew it would appeal to you people and ease some of your worrying, so I gave it to you for what it was worth. The latest rumor is that Patton wanted us because we have a good reputation, and Patton gets what he wants. There are rumors and rumors. In any event, I hate combat, as does everybody else who's been in it, and I see little need for volunteering. It's very much like the outfit where the Sergeant says, "I want three volunteers for this detail --- you, you, and you."

Things are pretty quiet up here now, and I'm convinced that none of the work ahead of us will be anywheres near as tough as those hedgerows were. We've got observation for miles, and our superiority of tanks and Artillery can really be brought into play. As soon as our supply bases are moved forward and the logistics problems are solved, we'll be ready for that last big push. You'll know that the supply problem is well on its way to being solved when my mail begins to arrive regularly again. Don't worry about me --- after what I've sweated out, I'll make it the rest of the way.

Those Nazis are really crazy, though. Many of them actually still believe they can lick us. I read one of their Party political analysis of the situation. "The closer the Allies come to apparent victory," it said, "the more their contradictions will operate to destroy them. England is extremely annoyed and concerned at Russia's victories in the Balkans." They're still depending on the disruption of the United Nations. About all we get on the radio is the German stations, which are very close to us, and they're still issuing the old anti-Semitic arguments too. They have programs in English with American music and a Nazi's version of American humor --- all mixed in with their propaganda, and the concoction is the funniest thing you've ever heard.

Of course I know about the point system for discharging soldiers from the Army. And of course I'd clean up on it --- with my decorations, combat stars, and all. But that system applies only to enlisted men. Can you see them discharging Infantry officers while we're still at war with Japan? No, the plan is that officers will be discharged only when their services are no longer needed.

We just heard that the Poles fighting in Warsaw have had to give up. They will no doubt all be killed. One of the terrible things about war is that even in victory there are set-backs, and many good men have to die.

The Maginot line isn't all it was cracked up to be --- I can now assure you. Siegfried neither.

I don't really mind your going out with those characters in Greenwich Village if you have a good time. But they better not make any passes. No kidding. I can get very angry.

I've got a feeling I'm going to have a lot of fun laying Artillery fire on the Germans when we get up on line. That BC scope we captured at St. Joseph will really come in handy. It has a magnification of 20X. We'll really be able to pick up the bastards with that. ...

***

Wed. nite, Oct. 4, 1944

Europe

Dear Dopey:

My good luck is continuing. Got 5 (five) letters from you today. That Danny character still annoys me, now that I've had some more information about him. If he's a broker or something, then why isn't he in the Army? He certainly sounds healthy enough. I've gotten so used to thinking of all normal men being in the war, with a few reasonable exceptions like Larry, that it kind of burns me up to hear of all those phonies running around loose in night clubs and summer resorts, and chasing after the wives of men who are fighting the war. How do all those cowboys and night club friends of Sherry's manage to dodge the draft so successfully?

Oh, well. I sure am getting tired of the war. Those Nazi bastards. However, don't mind me. I'm just a grouch, and I'm jealous because I can't do all those things and go to all those places --- not jealous of your going out, but of all those guys who ought to be here and not there. As long as I'm letting down my hair, I might mention that the way you spent that night when you told your mother you were at Sherry's doesn't go over so big with me. You see, I'm getting socially reactionary in my old age. I wish I were home, though. A girl can't wait for a guy forever.

People say combat is toughest when you go back to it after a long rest. Guys who were hit and get repaired at hospitals and were then returned to the front say that it's much harder than it was the first time. It's like you with your vacation. The office is even worse than it was before the vacation. *C'est la vie.* There are worse things. I can take anything as long as I keep getting your letters. I can understand, though, that you didn't have as much time or inclination to write during vacation as you did before. I expected that. But now you'll turn them out long and regularly, won't you baby?

***

At night -- Friday, Oct. 6, 1944

Europe

Dear Dopey:

There are planes overhead, and I just said, "Them planes is enemy planes, on account of they go mmmMMMmmmMMM." That has become a standing gag in this outfit. There are a lot of people who always come out with the analysis that certain planes are enemy because they can "tell by the sound." They are usually the same people who say that every round of artillery that lands on them is an 88, and every stray bullet that whistles by is fired by a sniper. Oh, well.

All I got in the mail today was another post card of yours from that horse place, and three packages, including one from you, and two from my parents. We got paid today. Every new country we go to we get paid in a different kind of money, and we now carry three different types of money, French francs, Belgian francs, and German marks, and it's driving everybody whacky. When you buy a glass of beer in town it's absolutely impossible to figure out how much change you're supposed to get. But the civilians are so used to dealing in all those denominations that they figure it out in a jiffy. But you can't check on them. It would take a slide rule and around three hours of calculations. All very confusing.

Everybody is bitching because the United States has admitted 900 refugees from all the countries of Europe for the duration of the war. "That's what we're fighting for, blah, blah, blah," they say, pointing at the pictures in Life of all the bedraggled looking victims of Fascism, "--- so that we'll have to support all those people." Americans, and all other peoples, I guess, are so hopelessly chauvinistic that it's practically impossible to get a word in edgewise on this subject. It's much the same as the Negro question. Oh, well. You just can't challenge every prejudice people have. You have to wait for a propitious moment, or the whole crowd gangs up on you. It's happened plenty of times. As a matter of fact, I'm considered a sort of queer duck anyway, --- for knowing foreign languages, I guess.

I better go to bed. They want me to ask the lady who owns the house we live in if she has any eggs, and I want to get her before she goes to bed. The Colonel, the Executive Officer, Schmitt, and I share a room in their house, and of course I'm the interrogator, so I have to get the eggs.

I was up at the front line units today, and saw a funny but so typically American G.I. scene --- a soldier lying at the bottom of his hole and reading Yank magazine. The Germans pooped a few rounds in this morning, and produced a few casualties, so all the boys have become believers and dug their holes deeply, but that doesn't stop them from keeping up on their literature. When we were fighting we used to get Stars and Stripes pretty regularly. In a way war is a very funny institution.

We're going to bed. Do you like me still? Or have you forgotten all about me? Remember me? Your husband. So long you dopey face.

***

Tonite is Monday, Oct. 9, 1944

Europe (Somewhere)

Dear Dopey:

I've come a long way since I landed on the coast of France nearly 4 months ago. I've seen Krautland. This is a pretty quiet sector, though. Very little doing, except patrolling.

We've been picking up a lot of Russian workers lately. This evening I had a 17 year old kid from some place in the Ukraine. My Russian has gotten somewhat rusty. My German is a good deal better than my Russian by now, whereas before the war it was the other way around.

I'm getting awfully tired of this kind of life. I've been feeling very irritable lately. Lost a good boy the other day. Used to be my Intelligence Sergeant. He never knew what hit him. But he's the only casualty we've had in the Battalion since we got up here, so you can see how quiet it is. On this kind of terrain you just have to use your head and keep from exposing yourself.

The Moselle river was the border between us and the enemy. We had to set up a defensive position on the Luxembourg side, and across the river was Germany. Before emplacing the Companies, it was necessary to reconnoiter our side of the line. I divided the sector into two parts, and assigned Tom Baxter, my Sergeant, the left half. He took my jeep and driver and two of our men. I took the other jeep and drove off to explore the right half. When I got to the river I could see that the road followed the shore line and that stretches of it were exposed to the enemy on the other side. So I decided to do the rest of the reconnaissance on foot, which meant following the wooded area along our side of the road. It took several hours, including time to get back to the jeep afterwards. When I finally returned to Battalion, Baxter was dead. He had chosen to make the reconnaissance driving down the road, and caught the entire burst of machine gun fire in his chest. No one else in the jeep was hit.

I was very shaken. Baxter had been married exactly two weeks before leaving for overseas. I promised myself to look up his wife in Florida after the war. But somehow I never did, and it has been on my conscience ever since. The period of mourning is short in combat, and after a couple of days I promoted my driver Smitty to Staff Sergeant.

Boy, am I tired of the Army. I wouldn't mind the fighting so much if it weren't for all the c.s. when we're not fighting.

Everybody's playing poker except me. I'm writing dopey a letter. The weather is cold and damp. We all have colds. Fooey. Why don't those silly Nazis call it a war? I've really got nothing to write about.

We got a wounded prisoner the other night. He was hit pretty bad. I spoke to him while they were giving him a blood transfusion at the Bn. Aid Station. He was one of those young Nazi bastards. He kept begging me to give him his Iron Cross --- it was in the pocket of his jacket with all his papers. I found the Iron Cross, as well as the orders awarding it to him. He had just gotten it. "In the name of the Führer," it said, "P.f.c. --- --- is hereby awarded the Iron Cross, Second Class." There were also a lot of snapshots of his girl Hedy. "Can't I please have my Iron Cross?" he kept saying. "You'll get a wooden one if you don't shut up," I told him. He was only semi-conscious, and became delirious --- started muttering, "We've got to get back, we've got to get back." I got his slimy, sticky blood all over me. After I was through questioning him they evacuated him in an ambulance. I don't know whether he died or not --- he was shaking like a leaf --- I forget whether that's caused by shock or loss of blood.

The Colonel insists on knowing what the hell I have to write about so much. He says you're a wonderful wife to send me so many packages. He's got ten packages on the way, but never seems to be getting them.

Write me more letters you little dope. I'm going to bed. G'nite silly.

I'm enclosing a copy of a leaflet we served Hitler's children. There's another language that's a lot more convincing, though.

What can I give you for an anniversary present? Better count the camera for that. There's another package you'll be getting around that time with German caramels and those earrings I got in Rennes, and the firing cap off the booby trap. But I'd rather count the camera as the main present. You're silly for insuring it, though. Nothing is worth that much money, except a man's life. And you can't make up for that with money. For us property is practically worthless. We lose it and find it every day. Why should anyone ever want to insure anything? What good is money anyway? Only life is important. Anyway, I'm awfully sorry I can't spend our second anniversary with you, dopey darling. I'll try to make the third. Gee, how old I'm getting.

***

Thur., Oct. 12, 1944

Dear Dopey:

I don't feel like writing, because I'm so mad about the mail situation. The last letter from you was dated Sept. 28, and that was several days ago. I got a letter from Rivkie day before yesterday.

That's all. Nothing ever happens much, except that a few more Nazis get killed. I've seen Krautland, by the way --- the second milestone for me in this war. The first was my landing in France last June. It's been a long trip since I left you at Meade.

I reread your letter about your new job, seeing as how there are no new letters to read. It strikes me awfully funny how the personnel manager acted as though he were trying to sell you the idea of taking a job. My associations with personnel managers consist of little cards filled out, a few piercing looks and questions, and a curt remark, "We'll get in touch with you." Times sure have changed. Do you think they'll be changed back when I get home? The world is such a crazy place.

All we ever talk about is how soon the war will end. I guess it's the same with you people. We're inclined to be less enthusiastically optimistic than you. That's only natural because when there's a big victory all you read about is the victory, while we see the people left lying on the road. The mistake we make though is that we tend to base our judgment too much on the local picture. People here are a little disappointed at the Red Army for not tearing into East Prussia and Warsaw at the original pace, and pay little attention to the funny sounding strange Hungarian, Romanian, and Yugoslav names which show that the Russians never stopped, but merely shifted their offensive to places where they could break through more quickly.

I was obviously giving no thought to the possibility of political motives behind some strategic decisions.

This is a fundamental principle of tactics --- commit your reserves where the enemy is weakest. The amateur always thinks that just because the enemy has piled up concentrations of men and material in one place we've got to pile ours up in the same place. This is wrong, however. Victories are won by bypassing centers of resistance which are too strong, and probing for weak spots to pour through. Anyway, our people here think in terms of their own fronts, and read with great interest of Russian advances directly across from us on the other side of Germany, but take far less interest in little details like knocking out the Baltic and Balkan countries. Actually, it won't be long before practically all the fighting will be going on in Germany and Austria. I think the invasion of Austria is next on the program --- through Hungary. Anyway, from being optimistic about how soon the war will end, the boys have become over-pessimistic. I guess it's just as well, because when a soldier figures the war is about over, he's afraid to take any more chances.

But anyway, I think things are going quite well. Those silly Krauts.

***

V- mail: Oct. 14, 1944

Somewhere in Luxembourg

Dear Dopey:

The mail situation is so bad that not only are we getting no mail, but we can't even get any air-mail stamps. That's why I'm using the V-mail form.

There's nothing to write about anyway. We're now allowed to say that we're in Luxembourg. No doubt you've gathered that already though.

Anyway, there's plenty of beer. I'm drinking some right now. Do you know that I haven't had a drink of water in around three months?

What does water taste like anyway? So long, you silly no-writing wife you.

***

Sunday, Oct. 15, 1944

Somewhere in Luxembourg

Dear Dopey:

I'm driving everybody crazy around here moaning for mail. It's becoming practically a pathological obsession. You'd better get some mail to me *toute suite,* even if you have to bring it yourself.

I spent a whole morning shelling a house, just because some civilian told me there's a pill box under it and the house is just camouflage. It's awfully hard to reduce a solid stone building with Artillery --- that's really a job for the Air Corps. Artillery only puts holes in it, and even so most of the shells are likely to miss it entirely.

[The Colonel just arrived with the Regimental Commander, and I grabbed hold of some papers, trying to look busy. But the Regimental C.O. didn't come inside, and the Colonel entered alone. "Oh," I said. "It's only you. Then I don't have to make like I'm working." I'm telling you, baby face, that's the trouble with a quiet sector. You're liable to receive visits from Colonels and Generals who will heckle the heck out of you. It's a hell of a thing when a man can't even find peace and refuge from the brass hats at the front lines. As soon as the lead starts singing through the air, you know you're safe again.]

Anyway, when I shelled the house the day before, we were a little worried about mask clearance. The O.P. from which we were observing the target was directly between the battery and the target, and on high ground; so we weren't sure whether the shells would clear us and reach the target, or hit us first. We started by firing over and then creeping in, listening for the whistle of the shells in order to determine how close they were coming. When we finally searched back to the target, the rounds sounded so close that we ducked inadvertently every time one came over. But we made it.

I kept watching the building for Heinies to come running out of it screaming, but no such luck. I know they're in the vicinity, because we've seen them. However, I hate to expend all that ammunition when I'm not certain that I'm killing Nazis. The Artillery liaison officer always gives me a guilty conscience. I come in glowing with excitement. "Boy, we hit it all right!" "How many rounds?" he asks. I tell him. "Was it effective?" he asks. "Hell, yes, it was effective!" "Well," he says, counting on his fingers, "Let's see. Was it worth eight hundred bucks?" And then my conscience starts bothering me, and I figure that maybe I'm being a spendthrift, because after all you people back home have to pay for this stuff, and here I am tossing it around bang, bang, bang. So please forgive me for splurging so much of your dough. I really mean well. About all I spend my pay on is postage stamps, and now you can't even get those. But I'm as apt as not to spend around a year's pay in a couple of hours just tossing shells all over the Siegfried line. Wasteful! Gosh, this war sure costs money. Wow.

Anyway, buy yourself a nice present. I don't need a thing, except my Army discharge. If you can get me one of those for our second anniversary, it would be duly appreciated. Gosh, I bet you're cuter than hell, ain't you?

***

Tuesday, Oct. 17, 1944

Luxembourg

Dear Dopey:

Yesterday and today everybody but me got a whole slew of letters. "Well, what do you expect?" they say. "Don't you know what those dude ranches are like?" The Colonel says I shouldn't ream you too much, but I am very very angry. Boy, if I don't get a pack of mail tomorrow, all kinds of terrible things will happen. The Colonel got mail as recently dated as only eight days ago all the way from California. I would think you weren't writing because I look so funny with all my hair clipped off, but you can't see it. Anyway, there better be something tomorrow.

Have I ever told you some of the cities I was in in [*sic*] France? Paris is about the only big one I missed. I was in Carentan, Tours, Angers, Orleans, St. Malo, Dinard, Dinan, Rennes. I thought Angers and Rennes were the nicest. Tours was very beautiful when you got out of the business district, which wasn't particularly nice. The French girls were amazingly and consistently pretty, I guess because they know how to dress and make up. The Luxembourg girls are as consistently unattractive, probably for the same reason in reverse. But those French ones really had shapes on them. Everybody who bitched about France when we were there, now moans and wishes he were back. It's really a very nice country.

How do I know you even exist?

I wish the rainy weather would end. Too much mud. Mud and horse manure. That's all I see. I can't tell you what cities I've visited in this country, because it's so small that I might not be complying with censorship requirements about not revealing my location. But you can't get any gifts in the main city. Not a thing in the stores. As if I'd buy you anything anyway.

I think the Red Army will be invading Austria next. I want this war to end soon. You can't spend your whole life killing Germans. It's a helluva career.

I'm not writing any more. You don't deserve it. I don't know why I think about you so much.

P.S.: This is my last letter until I hear from you.

***

Wed. nite, Oct. 18, 1944

Luxembourg

Dear Dopey:

I have to write you today and apologize for that nasty letter I wrote last night. I got 5 letters from you today, dated July 25, Oct. 2, 4, 6, & 7. I knew it wasn't your fault that I hadn't received anything before, but I had to bitch to someone, and you were selected. I figured if I bitched enough the mail would get through, and it worked.

Now I've got things to write about. Give Carl all my love, He's really lucky not to have died, with the wound you said he had.

You can go right ahead having good times and not worrying about me, dopey. In the situation we're in now I'm just as safe as when I was back in the rear. We practically never receive any artillery fire --- only a few mortar rounds get pooped over on our outposts occasionally. We've had practically no casualties, but we've killed a lot of Krauts across the river. They run around like a bunch of lunatics, exposing themselves, and they build fires to cook their food --- the dopes. It's beautiful landscape, just like a shooting gallery. You know those places in Coney Island where ducks slide across a landscape background. Only the landscape is Germany and the ducks are a bunch of silly Nazis. Every time they expose themselves we throw artillery at them, and instead of lying down and taking cover, they run like hell, and we put fire on them right out in the open. I can't understand that psychology. Whenever somebody shoots at me I always hit the ground and try to force my body into the earth. You'd be surprised at the things I can take cover behind. The shrapnel can sing all around, but it passes over, as do the bullets. But I can't understand these dumb Krauts. They're young Nazi kids --- inexperienced and full of zip until they get really frightened. Then they just get up and run --- that's when you can kill them best. It's a very one-sided scrap. Very safe for our side, and costly for them. *This would not last, unfortunately.* It's a rather slow way of getting home though, and I wish the next D-day would come soon. I believe it will be the last.

N. is rather a disappointment to me. He has been from the time he decided to take that 4F job in the Air Corps instead of trying to go to war. I guess he's completely domesticated by now. Oh, where are the snows of yesteryear? I feel as young as I did eight years ago, but my friends are growing old.

> *Infantryman's macho would surge when we were no longer the ones who were dying. Short memories preserved our sanity. I would not talk or think like that when I would again lie cursing in a slit trench, waiting for each incoming shell to crash to earth, wondering oh God will this be me, and hearing the screams of the wounded, and wanting only to be out of there.*

I'm glad to hear that Sol S. is in France, and that Carl P. is going soon. I'm sorry he's not in the Infantry though. Carl would really make a swell doughboy. The Artillery is a good branch, but except for the Forward Observers, they don't even know there's a war going on.

> *We would laugh at the newspaper headlines that spoke of "Artillery duels." An Artillery duel, we would say, is when each side shells the other side's Infantry.*

The Germans don't have enough Artillery to get any effective counter-battery fire, so it's almost like being in the rear --- a strictly technical job. But very important nevertheless. I realize now what a weapon the Artillery is for us. It works strictly for the Infantry. We fire it just as if it were a rifle. They shoot at anything we tell them to. I always used to think that Artillery was a branch of service. But it isn't. It's a weapon. And the Artillerists work for us. If a machine gun is holding you up, all you do is find it and call for fire. Within one or two minutes it's delivered.

It's too bad that W. had to get stuck in the Transportation Corps. That's considered one of the biggest rackets in the Army. They get extra pay and have absolutely nothing to do but ride back and forth. I know somebody has to do things like that, but it seems to me there are plenty of old people, without inactivizing [*sic*] intelligent young people like Milt. Some silly medic ruined him for the war effort right at the inception of his career. His vision is no worse than mine or Carl's. It's just one of those ridiculous technicalities. But I know it's no fault of his. I suspect he didn't talk much about his job because there's nothing to talk about. It's just a well-paying rut.

Most soldiers have a great deal of contempt for button-boy soldiers, and in some cases it's well justified, because there are a lot of them who want nothing better than to be safe and comfortable.

I've learned one big mistake I made, incidentally, --- and that was turning down that instructor's job at Benning. Our best people here are former Benning instructors. My Colonel is one, and a couple of the Company Commanders. And they really know their stuff. I'd certainly have been better off if I'd taken that job. But you can't always make the right decision, after all. I'm not a professional soldier, and the only time I can tolerate the Army is in combat. At all other times it gets under my skin. Anyway, I've learned enough so that if at some time in the future I have to buckle that pistol belt around my waist again I'll know what the score is.

Give Miltie my love. I sure wish we could have him out here. He has just the kind of level head it takes. There's only one thing I can't stand, and that's nervous people. We've got one nervous officer in the Battalion, and he really gets to me. He looks just like Peter Lorre, and has a terrible persecution complex. He was evacuated as a battle fatigue casualty back in the early days, but he raised such a fuss that he made them send him back. Normally battle fatigue cases are never sent into combat again, and I respect him for fighting to get back. Battle fatigue is what they used to call shell shock in the last war. In plain language it's a form of insanity that comes about as a result of fear and horror. It's quite common in the Infantry. The symptoms usually are a complete nervous and physical breakdown. The man begins to cry like a baby, and starts shaking like a leaf. I saw it happen to an officer once, and it promptly happened to three men as soon as they saw him. It's very contagious. The medics have an excellent method of treating it. They cure the majority of cases, but they're obviously unfit for combat.

Oh, I forgot to tell you --- I just saw a movie this evening --- "Ladies in Washington," or some such nonsense. It brought Washington back to me. What a phony place that is --- seems like everybody there is a parasite sponging off the war. Anyway, you see what kind of sissy war we're fighting, when I can go to the movies. We're listening to the radio now, and drinking our whiskey ration, which arrived today. The most popular song on the radio is, "You May Grow Up to be a Fish." I think it's kind of cute. So are you. It has a moral too.

You misunderstand my "attitude" toward the Germans. I hate the bastards. It's just that I get annoyed at hearing the same song from the fellows all the time about how they'll run rampant, and I believe it's the wrong emphasis to assume that "punishing" or wiping out any nation will prevent war in the future. Fascism is not limited to Germany, and only the correct international post-war policy will prevent future wars, not killing a lot of women and children. That's just hysteria, not common sense. Of course I agree with you in everything you say about Germany being reduced in strength and dismembered until it is ready to be received again in the family of nations. But this business of killing everyone over 15 is nonsense. In the first place it will never be done. In the second place saying things like that is just grist in Hitler's propaganda machine. It really gives them something to fight for, since they will then have nothing to lose. Certainly the whole people is responsible, and must pay for their crimes, but everybody seems to think that the destruction of Germany is synonymous with the preservation of peace, and that just isn't so. How about Spain and Italy and all the other little countries with reactionary rulers? It seems to me that the most important thing is the same old collective security, the lack of which was directly responsible for this war. It may be some other country 20 years from now, and all that's necessary is that anybody that starts up again be stepped on while the stepping is easy. Germany is by this time a big boil on the face of the earth. It has to be lanced and bled until the bad blood is all gone. But that's incidental compared with the need for seeing that the infection doesn't break out somewhere else.

That's all I meant. I'm no milquetoast. I can kill a man as easily as you swat a fly when there's good reason for it. But a lot of irresponsible threats which will never be carried out do no one any good, and I don't have to whip myself up into an anti-German frenzy in order to fight. I can keep my perspective and still do it.

Incidentally, don't forget that the seeds of fascism exist in many countries, including our own, and I don't believe, as many seem to think, that Nazism is a strictly German affair. Wiping out nations isn't the cure for it. I think, as you do, that Germany has to be thoroughly weakened until all the bad blood is cleaned out, but that's purely incidental to the question of what our post-war policy will be. It's the emphasis I disagree with. People say that the reason the war broke out is that we didn't wipe out Germany after the last one, and that's nonsense, as you well know. I hope I've made myself clear now.

I hope there's more mail from you tomorrow, pie face. I don't at all believe that I would feel awkward with you, like Carl with Sherry. I could take up right where I left off with the greatest of ease. You just wait around..

The Colonel just looked over my shoulder, and said, "Six pages, Jesus Christ, what does he write about." He spent the day zeroing his new rifle, and he's going down to snipe at the Germans with it tomorrow. He's a character.

Good night, you silly sophisticated baby. Go on having fun. I'm in no danger, except that I slipped today on my hob-nailed shoes, and nearly broke my neck.

***

Friday, Oct. 20, 1944

Luxembourg

Dear Dopey:

We spent a morning down at the shooting gallery teaching the Germans military tactics. The unfortunate thing about these lessons is that the students are usually no longer in a position to put their experience to any use after the instruction is over. We were dropping mortar shells on an open field which, incidentally, had a couple of haystacks on it. One of the rounds happened to hit one of the stacks, and to our surprise, instead of just a lot of wisps of straw being blown apart, out come a bunch of Krauts running as fast as Hitler down Delancey Street. They were right out in the open, and there wasn't a bush or tree for hundreds of yards around. Our machine guns opened up on them, and they hit the ground so fast we couldn't tell whether they were killed or just scared to death. So we started laying in more mortar and artillery time fire. As soon as the shelling would stop, some of them would get up and run again, and the machine guns let them have another burst. You've really missed something if you haven't seen a bunch of Nazi supermen running for their lives. Finally a couple of them staggered into the second "haystack," and we started laying 105 mm. artillery on it. When we finally got a direct hit, the shell just bounced off the haystack! So we fired some more, and enough of the hay was ripped off to reveal the pillbox underneath. We couldn't even chip it with 105's, but that isn't all there is in the U.S. Army, so I'm afraid the Siegfried line will just have to manage with one or two fewer pillboxes.

I think the first haystack had a dugout and hasty emplacement, but the second one was one of those concrete and steel jobs.

It's fun to be shooting at Germany though, instead of one of the occupied countries. The terrain is the type we learned about in Ft. Benning --- no more of this hedgerow country. If you use your head you live to a ripe old age; if you don't you may not.

I had absolutely no sense of identification with the enemy. Otherwise I might have remembered the complete terror of the time when it was I who was the deer caught in the headlights. It was shortly after we got out of the hedgerows and broke into the open. I had never faced a German tank before. Its gun swung around, pointed directly at a Company Commander some 20 yards to my right and fired a shell point blank, blowing him and his radio operator to pieces. It then started coming around toward me, and I pressed myself to earth as hard as I could, waiting for death to come. But instead the gun passed me by.

When I looked up again the turret had returned to its forward position, and the tank moved on.

Guess what. We just got a report from one of the Companies. The Germans have moved a P.A. system up on the other side of the river, and have started asking us to surrender. "Do you want to be home for Christmas?" they asked. But they didn't get to finish their sentence, because of all the artillery and mortar fire that dropped in on them.

"Well," the Company Commander asked me. "Shall I surrender?"

"Sure," I said. "If they can guarantee that we'll be home for Christmas."

They must be completely nuts, these squareheads. We spend the whole day killing them, and at night they ask us if we want to surrender. They are completely out of their heads. You ought to hear their radio broadcasts. They announce the news of all their defeats in such a cheerful way that a man from Mars would think they're winning the war. I tell you, dopey, I've seen all the wonders of the world by this time.

What do you think, baby face? Should we surrender? It's been officially announced today that the invasion of the Philippines is on, and the Germans say the Russians are in East Prussia, and Aachen has fallen. *That city would come to have a special significance for me.* So the Germans cheerfully ask us if we're ready to surrender now. What are you going to do with people like that? You can't kill them all. There isn't enough ammunition. So you kill nine out of ten, and the tenth one clicks his heels and demands that you give up.

The picture I'm sending you was taken in our area near *Chateau-le-Veliere,* about 40 kilometers from Tours. It's a pretty crumby picture, I don't really look that bad. But it's of no use to me, so I'm sending it to you.

How did the films come out? Let me know, and I'll tell you what they were about. They were all taken around Dinard. One of them is a picture of the Citadel of St. Malo just after it had fallen, and the Stars and Stripes had just been hoisted.

I took a hot bath in a tub today.

Those stories about the cities along the Rhine having all their lights on when our planes went over are just as crazy as this business of the Germans asking us to surrender. I think the whole country is just plain nuts. What do you think? G'nite pieface.

***

Thursday nite, Oct. 26, 1944

Luxembourg

Dear Dopey:

You ought to be getting this letter just about in time for our second anniversary. It's silly to congratulate you, so what in hell am I to say? You know how it is. Here I am and there you are, and not a goddam thing I can do about it. Just keep killing Nazis? What a lifetime career for a grown man. And what a way to spend our second anniversary. However, ---

No, Blood and Guts isn't working me any more. I quit his Army the other day. We're in the First now. Seems like we change Armies every couple of weeks. Like the classic Benning answer to all questions, it depends on the situation and the terrain.

I dug out the copy of Ehrenberg's writings that you sent me a long time ago. At the time I received it we were in the middle of a battle, so I just stuffed it away somewhere. However, I read it yesterday, and left it lying around, so everybody else is reading it now. The Colonel reads everything he gets his hands on. I waited for his usual classic comment. He read several articles, and then said, "Hmm, these Russians seem to be mad about something." We've been getting a lot of stuff lately on the big picture in our G-2 reports, and in today's report there's a story on the treatment of Russian war prisoners in German concentration camps, specifically those who had been identified as Communist Party members. They beat and starved them, as usual, and wanted to have them shot, but for some reason the German soldiers seemed to rebel at the idea, and wouldn't shoot. So the prisoners were moved into nice clean new barracks, and several were interviewed and examined by German doctors, who prescribed milk diets, etc., for the starved prisoners. When asked why they were in such poor health, the Russians explained that they had been given nothing to eat. It looked like they were to receive very humane treatment, and everyone was impressed. Each Russian prisoner was to receive a complete physical checkup, and they were lined up. In the first room was a big white table with all kinds of medical supplies, and there was a medic with a Red Cross armband, who asked very solicitous medical questions and made entries in his book. They were then marched to another room, one by one, and stepped up on a scale, where height and weight was measured. As they stood on the scale, the killer observed the exact height of the victim and fired a pistol from a fixed mount through a slit in the wall, hitting the prisoner in the back of the neck. Around the scale was a bathtub arrangement, so that after each man was killed, the blood was washed away, and each new victim found a nice clean room when he came in and stepped up on a scale. Five hundred men were shot in this manner.

Well. Early this morning two soldiers in German uniforms strolled unarmed into one of our towns. As soon as they saw our men they clasped their hands behind their heads in the approved position of the German soldier when surrendering. They turned out to be Silesian Poles who had deserted while on patrol. They said they would be willing to lead me back across the river to where their buddies were. All the Poles wanted to surrender, and a lot of Germans too. But the Colonel figured it didn't pay to go after that. Let them come here.

Anyway, they told us everything --- Battalion C.P., Company C.P., all the positions, etc., etc. We now know every little detail about their lives over there. So right this minute our Artillery is roaring whoom-whom-whoom! We begin in the rear of the German lines, where their kitchen train is. Then our Artillery is searching down the road which the horse-drawn chow trucks use as they carry the chow down through Battalion and Company C.P.'s. At Company the food is hand-carried by representatives from each squad down to the front-line positions. Our Artillery is following this whole process down the line, ending up by firing concentrations on the front line positions and the C.P.'s. In other words, we are feeding Fritz hot chow tonight. I hope he enjoys it.

You see we have a little debt to repay. Back in Normandy the Germans seemed to know just the time when our kitchens brought up supper, and their Artillery would lay right in on us. Every meal cost us several casualties. The men would have to leave their holes to get chow, and that's when the Artillery fire would catch them. After a couple such meals we decided we'd rather eat K-rations and have the same number of men alive after supper as before. You'd be surprised how such experiences dull the appetite. Anyway, we're paying them back now. It's hot chow in Germany tonight.

I'm sorry about the dopey letter I wrote you about your 4-F (?) friend Danny the stock broker. I got your letter of Sept. 17 only a couple of days ago, in which you explained about him in the first place. For some reason that letter was long delayed, and all the others I received kept talking about your going out with him, like you had been doing it for months, and I didn't know what missing links to supply. Overseas mail delivery is apt to produce many silly things like that. Please don't be mad at me.

I think you'll get too smart for your pants soon. You'll know all about the practical end of engineering, and I won't know nuthin', except how to kill Krauts, and there won't be any left by that time, so wot'l I do, become a gangster?

Those ole Russians. Imagine them invading Norway too. I asked those two Silesians how much they knew about the world situation. They didn't know about the Russians being in East Prussia, and they became very excited when I told them about Norway. They said practically everybody in their outfit knows that Germany is losing the war. But they don't know just what to do about it. Morale is pretty low. It's a *Volksdeutsch* outfit --- which means non-Germanic peoples for the most part --- so it's no indication of what goes on in the mind of the "pure" Aryan. But I think they all know it by now.

So long cutie.

***

Friday, Oct. 27, 1944

Luxembourg

Dear Dopey:

I got three letters today, all dated Oct. 15. One was from you, one from Irv Heymont, & one from my parents. Irv's letter consisted merely of a copy of the mimeographed order containing my letter to him. It's a Division order, and says that the letter speaks for itself, and will be read to all units by an officer and posted on bulletin boards. I don't mind his having used it, because my name doesn't appear, and there's no danger of my being embarrassed. It was an interesting letter, and reading it now was like reading somebody else's stuff published in "Battle Experiences." I'd forgotten what I had written. The very personal stuff had been omitted and all names deleted. Also it was censored in at least one place, where I said, "Since you've landed a juicy assignment at Benning School for Boys." It was changed to read, "Since you've landed at Benning." It wasn't a bad letter at all, and I learned a lot from reading it.

Solly is right about the pictures in the Leica. I didn't take any of those you sent me. None of my friends wear German uniforms. Before I read your letters I was a little puzzled at the pictures. I recognized the background as the harbor at St. Malo and Dinard. But I knew I hadn't taken the pictures. When I read your letter I understood. I guess I ruined all the pictures I took. There were a lot of me. But apparently the only ones that came out were the ones the Kraut took. It's funny seeing all those places with Krauts instead of G.I.'s running around. The picture of the little lighthouse out on the water has in the background the island of Cezembre, which doubtlessly you know all about now. The picture next to the one showing a life preserver hanging between two soldiers' heads is of the Citadel. The boat scenes were taken on the ferry which ran between St. Malo and Dinard. I saw the railroad with the tracks and cars all blown up too. That was in Dinard.

Of course I never stopped loving you, dopey. What a silly dream. You're a dope.

I am eating a Hershey bar and drinking a bottle of wine. What are you doing?

War is hell. If we don't have that movie tomorrow I'll go crazy with boredom.

I'm getting awfully tired of this stuff. I'm kind of banking on a big crack-up after election. What you said about the possibility of the Nazis holding out till they see who wins the election is not altogether ridiculous. It's not only a question of being able to find a haven in South America if Dewey is elected. They probably figure that if Dewey is elected they can have some kind of armistice and a better peace. If he's elected and they hold out till he's inaugurated, they'll certainly be better off than if Roosevelt is President. But I'm afraid that even in this the Nazis haven't a chance. Everybody as usual is playing poker tonight for thousands of francs as stakes, but nobody was willing to put up any money on Dewey's election. Anyway, I did my part for the war. I cast my vote for F.D.R. Now let's see some results.

Don't let those big fat draft dodgers grab all the seats in the subway and keep you from writing me. I'm really feeling the lack of your letters.

No kidding. This war gotta end. They're overdoing it. I'm getting very angry.

I wanna go home.

I'm not even doing any fighting hardly. I'm tired of having the Regimental Commander come around and ask me a lot of damn fool questions.

***

Sunday, Oct. 29, 1944

Luxembourg

Dear Dopey:

I've been feeling rather low lately, I guess mainly because I'm not doing anything, and since you stopped getting seats in the subway you don't bother to write me very often. ...

Interesting current events column (local)

1. A German pilot who got war-weary flew his plane over to our side and landed it on one of our airfields, giving himself up.

2. A German Major in civvies who was supposed to be spying also got tired of it all and turned himself in.

Looks like a long winter. I hope the Nazis all die of boredom, among other things. A lot of Germans are getting smart, and take the first opportunity to surrender. But there are still plenty of the other type.

People have gotten wind of the fact that you call me dopey, and when they see me writing you, they say, "Hey dopey, come home."

We're even out of liquor and wine. I just took a sip of water --- I swear to God --- it's the first drop of water I've had in four months.

You!

***

Sat'y nite, Nov. 4, 1944

Luxembourg

Dear Dora:

Today I sat around for several hours waiting for the mail orderly, who finally brought another batch of mail. This time there was some for me --- three letters, one from Rivka and two from my parents. The last letter took only 8 days getting here. It seems that when people bother to write, mail does manage to get through. Apparently you haven't found time to write me very often since you haven't been finding seats in the subway. I'm not saying you don't write at all. You probably do occasionally, and I'll be getting mail a couple of times a month --- in which case I'll answer just about that often. Surely in your busy day there must be some time to write me.

Maybe you think that since the element of physical danger is a lesser factor back home than it is over here, your letters don't mean as much. But that's where you're wrong. And when I get mail from everyone but you, it's just like those days when you never cared about me at all.

I'm so disgusted I don't care what happens to me anymore. I'm becoming irritable, and everything and everyone gets on my nerves. I'm sorry I have to take it out on you. But you're responsible in some measure.

Those goddam stinking Nazis are apparently going to see to it that as many of our boys are killed as possible before Germany falls. The way I'm beginning to feel now, it's O.K. with me if every last German is killed. I'm beginning to get a more intense personal satisfaction every day out of seeing dead Germans.

Today's Stars and Stripes has as its editorial an article by Ilya Ehrenburg on the cordial welcome with which the population of German towns are receiving American troops, in hope that since Americans haven't suffered from German atrocities they can be won over. He says, "The Americans have come to Germany not to pat child-slayers on the head or feed SS scoundrels with spam. The Americans have come to the land of gangsters in order to bring villains to justice. It is not only American Divisions that have entered Germany. Justice has entered Germany, and not a single German will venture to cry 'welcome' to justice. For justice carries a sword."

Anyway, that's got nothing to do with the original subject of your not writing me. Is six months so long that I'm no longer a part of your life?

I hope I'm being unjust to you, dopey, and that it's just another SOS screwup. In which case please forgive me.

***

Wed., Nov. 8, 1944

Luxembourg

Dear Dopey face:

I just got your letter of Oct. 28, which is counter-battery fire in reply to that first nasty letter I wrote you about the mail situation. I shudder to think what you will say when you receive the second nasty letter, which is much worse than the first. Gee, darling, I feel like an awful skunk. I didn't really mean any of the things I said. It was just a way of letting off steam, and insuring that I get mail the next day. And it worked. But I should have realized that it was liable to make you so mad. Please forgive me. It's just a trick to make the mail arrive the next day. But I deserve to have my ass reamed for doing it. ...

Maybe I've developed a crazy sense of humor out here. I remember lots of times whenever a shell whipped past and whoomed into the ground, kicking up a lot of dirt, but missing everybody, and we all tried to dive into the same foxhole at the same time. We'd all laugh like hell. I'd never have said all those things if I had figured you'd take it so seriously. Bitching is a tradition in the army. We always gotta bitch, to let off steam.

I just reread your letter again. Oh, what a heel I am. You poor kid. I ought to buy you a nice big present to console you for having married me, but all they've got in this part of the country is manure. All day long they shovel it from one place to another, and when they're through they start shoveling it right back to the first place. I can't understand how it works out, but everybody seems to make a living out of it.

Please like me again, dopey face.

Your big stinker of a husband.

***

Sat'y, Nov. 11, 1944

Luxembourg

Dear dopey baby:

I feel so lousy about what I've done to upset you so much. I promise never to do anything like that again. Please get some of my letters. I never stopped writing you, regardless of my "threats."

Well, anyway, you know how small I feel now. Today I got 3 letters from you. I'm paying for my follies. If only you don't get so mad at me that you never want to see me again. I'll just have to sweat it out.

Everybody sort of had a faint wishful hope that Germany would collapse today because of the date. But apparently no dice. Those bastards. I've just acquired a brand new M-1 rifle, and I hope to make good use of it. I'm just in the mood to draw a bead on a couple of Krauts.

It sure was nice to get some mail from you again. Keep writing me lots of letters. But promise me you won't feel upset if you don't hear for a while, and I'll try to do the same. Because that's what's going to happen. I feel thoroughly chastened. So long, babyface.

***

Monday, Nov. 13, 1944

Luxembourg

Dear dopey face:

I got two letters today, Nov. 1 & 3. I took a hot bath, and feel very lazy.

Some practical joker of a Major just emptied a bottle of liquor on the floor under my chair and tossed a lighted match on it. I was engrossed in writing this letter, and noticed nothing except how warm the room was getting. "Where is all that heat coming from?" I kept saying, until I happened to look down and notice that the floor was on fire under

199

me. What a waste of good liquor. But I guess it's all right, since they're washing themselves with champagne in one of the towns, and flushing the toilets with it. But that's a heluva thing to do with good Scotch whiskey.

Oh, well, you've got to pass the time somehow. The whole trouble with war is you're always either getting shot or bored to death. I don't know which is worse. I guess boredom is not as permanent in its effect, though.

I got a V-mail letter from Normie M. today, dated July 6. He was still in Nebraska on some Air Corps administrative job. It's funny how so many of my friends have found themselves nice soft jobs in the Air Corps --- Norm, Nate, Frank. At least Normie seems to have a sort of guilty conscience about it. He's proud of having been in the Infantry, but can't seem to help being glad he got out of it. He seems to know the score, though.

Not smug and self-satisfied as Nate and Frank appear to be. Oh, hell, why should I be so critical. I suppose all kinds of jobs are necessary. Still it always seems funny to me when a big healthy guy says, "At present I am doing a lot of good work crewing, classifying, selecting and assigning ground and air crews for the heavy bombers." Normie's O.K., though. He says his brother is overseas as a motion picture operator.

Hello, pieface. You still mad at me for writing you nasty letters? Hope there's more mail tomorrow. I like when I get mail. So long, you darling baby you.

***

Wed., Nov. 15, 1944

Hotel Windsor, --- , Luxembourg

Dear Dopey:

I find myself back in the rear somewhat today. Last night, for the first time since last April, I slept between sheets. You can't imagine the sensation. At first it felt ice cold on my bare legs, but after a few seconds the sheets became deliciously warm, and all I had was two blankets over me. That's what a difference a bed makes. When you sleep on the ground or the floor you can have lots of blankets and still freeze. In the morning my bed was made by a chambermaid.

This town is a famous summer resort. The borders of three countries come together here. People need to come here for the hot mineral baths. Tomorrow maybe I will take a hot mineral bath. Now all the hotels are full of soldiers. This is a real town, not full of cowflop like the little villages we used to be in.

I guess this is supposed to be a rest, but actually we do more work when we're in reserve than when we're on the line. Now we have to do training all day, while at the front there's nobody to bother you except the Germans. They don't bother us much. Occasionally they send a patrol over, and when they do they usually get so badly shot up that they keep away for several nights afterwards. They don't do much shooting from their positions, for fear of exposing themselves. Every time they fire Artillery or mortars we throw so much stuff back at them that they wish they had kept quiet in the first place.

Anyway, now we've gotta train and stuff. However, the surroundings are much nicer than previously, and sleeping between clean sheets in a modern hotel room rather appeals to me.

I've been filling up on beer and champagne this evening. Hey, funny face. Today's my birthday --- and I'm only 27. Hell, that's nothing. Most people are older than that. We've been married two years, but most of this time by remote control. When will I get to see you again, huh? All I've gotta do is get a compound leg fracture, or something. Another way is for the war to end.

Right across from where my hotel is you're in France. But this hotel is in Luxembourg.

Life is dull. Nothing ever happens to me. Does anything ever happen to you? People are getting leaves to Paris, but only a very few at a time. Maybe it will get around to me, eventually. 48 hours in Paris --- *nom de Dieu.*

I think I will take the elevator up to my room, and climb between those nice clean sheets. Why ain't you in between them too?

The Colonel says, "Tell your wife that if she doesn't send some books to read I'm gonna ship you back to Brooklyn." Send me eating stuff. *Gute nacht, liebchen.*

***

Thursday, Nov. 23, 1944

Thanksgiving in Luxembourg

Dear Dopey:

Last night we had our Battalion dance right here at the hotel, and it was very nice. We had a G.I. band which was *tres bon,* and everything to drink and sandwiches. The Luxembourg girls aren't so hot on this jitterbug stuff, but that doesn't bother the officers. Everybody had a good time. Practically no one got too drunk --- although of course there were the usual one or two. One of the Company Commanders got loaded, got hold of the daughter of the Minister of Justice, and was throwing her all over the dance floor. We figured that ought at least to cause an international incident. The girl said of him, "All the time he talk to me, but what he said it is not reasonable. He ask me for my address --- if he come to my house my mother will throw him out with me together."

The only casualties were two broken wine glasses and an aquamarine stone lost out of the ring of one of the girls, but that was found this morning. The girl of the aquamarine stone started getting cloyingly chummy, and I congratulate myself on the apparent success with which I made a disengaging movement merely by dropping the remark that I was married, and showing her pictures of my wife. "It's wonderful," I was thinking. "All you have to do is let yourself get hooked by one girl, and you're as safe as you want to be from all the others." But the setback to her morale was only a temporary one. She recovered

202

quickly, and pursued the attack with renewed effort. Anyway, either because I wasn't drunk enough, or she wasn't pretty enough, or it was raining too hard (seems to be raining most of the time these days), I finally put my food down and walked her home in the rain, while the rest of her family was being taken home in the Colonel's sedan.

I think the war is going O.K. Maybe not much longer to sweat it out. It's just a question of how disorganized the German situation is under the effects of all the powerful attacks now going on. They haven't the reserves it takes. Either they have to commit them piecemeal, in which case they are ineffectual, or else commit them in one sector and face disaster in the others. We just beat them to the punch. Our offensive started just as they were racing to get their counter-offensive going. It's really remarkable how well we are doing in view of the weather conditions. A couple of weeks of good weather might end it once and for all.

In fact the enemy did have reserves, and we would be meeting them soon.

I don't even know what terms we are on. The last letter I got from you, the one of Nov. 6, you were very mad at me. I just have to keep on writing without knowing whether you're getting my mail or not. Gee, dopey, stop being sore. I write you lots of letters.

P.S. I'll tell you what to send me, in addition to things to eat. Grease pencils, preferably red and blue. You can't get these things for love or money around here, and we really need them.

Friday, Nov. 17, 1944

Same hotel, --- , Luxembourg

Dear Dopey:

I'm getting so I can speak German very freely. I wish I had as much chance to use my Russian as I do German. I'm taking a trip to Luxembourg city to get some champagne.

The landlord's wife and the two chambermaids have just been standing here kidding around with me. "Tell your wife," they say, "that the Luxembourger women are very happy with the Americans --- that the Americans have liberated us, and that after the war the Boche will be this high," (holding the palm of the hand about one foot off the ground). The landlord's wife is rather good looking. After I had to guess her age, she turned out to be 30, has a 7 year old son --- but looks a lot younger. A good-looking woman is more or less a rarity in this country. In France pretty girls are as common as the leaves on the trees. I guess it's matter of dress and make-up, more than anything else. In France all the women on the streets wear bright and stylish clothes --- in Luxembourg they only get dressed up on Sundays.

Gee, dopey, being alive is really a lot of fun --- I sure am glad I'm still alive. ... I think I'll go up now and crawl between my nice clean sheets. Good night, sweetie pie.

***

Sat'y nite, Nov. 18, 1944

Luxembourg

Dear Dopey darling:

I got your Nov. 6 denunciation today. You're as certain in that letter that I'm deliberately not writing you as I was certain that you were neglecting writing me. The circumstantial evidence was fully as imposing. Boy, oh boy, a little old misunderstanding sure takes a lifetime to iron out with this ---- up mail service.

I went to Luxembourg today, and spent the afternoon shopping for presents. I found you a pretty sheer silk scarf, which comes from Belgium, and also a silly belt made of wooden beads. I got a simple little silver chain necklace for the Colonel to send his wife. Believe me, this was a real accomplishment. The stores in Luxembourg are almost completely empty. The windows have nothing but the pictures of the Duke and Duchess of Luxembourg, and a few paper decorations. I don't know why they even keep the stores open.

I was kind of afraid that the Colonel would try to take the scarf away to send his wife and leave me the necklace. I didn't even show him the scarf at first, and he was so surprised and pleased that I had actually gotten the necklace for him that he never even noticed the scarf. It's very sheer silk, and when my ex-driver Smitty saw it, he said "Boy, oh boy, would I like to see a girl dressed in nothing but that!" --- with which I heartily concur.

Unfortunately the package won't arrive in time to have any effect on my present situation. You still think all kinds of dopey things about me. I believe I told you about the guy who, after not getting a letter from his wife for a whole year, wrote her asking for a divorce, and got 186 letters the next day. What can I do, darling?

I've been talking to the people around here, and they've been telling me what the Germans did. They seemed particularly indignant over the way the Jews were treated --- there were a couple of thousand Jews in the Duchy. These Luxembourgers are fine people. It's the same old story. Nobody can understand why we treat the Germans so well. If we had only seen what they did, ---- .

Oh, dopey, please stop being mad at me. How many letters like that will I have to keep getting before the thing is cleared up? How do I know if you'll ever forgive me? Oh, dopey, please.

***

Monday, Nov. 20, 1944

Luxembourg

Dear Dopey:

About all we can get on the radio right now are the Kraut stations. They dominate most of the waveband. I just now got a Russian station. Some woman announcer was reading off a list of war decorations for heroism. Now I've got a station with American swing, which is all anybody ever wants to hear. I can never listen to symphony --- people always start squawking. This station I've got now --- there's no way of knowing if it's really an American station, or a Kraut station playing American music mixed in with the propaganda. No, it's a real American Forces broadcast. Just heard that the French First Army has reached the Rhine in the vicinity of Belfort. In fact, all our Armies are making advances, not with spectacular speed, but surely. If only we can get across the Rhine before midwinter, I think it will be the end. But that's a tall order.

I'm still living at the hotel. In fact, we're now engaged in preparations for our big dance a day after tomorrow. That, plus our temporary but nevertheless enticingly comfortable existence, has for the time being overshadowed our military pursuits. To tell you the truth I am not particularly eager to cover myself with glory. I wouldn't at all be disappointed if the war should be won without our ever being committed again. However, it will be as it must be. Regardless of what you may think, I really don't like war at all. People either get old before their time or die before they have a chance to. I'll tell you the most aging thing a man can do --- patrolling into the enemy lines.

Right now we're worrying about how to make up punch for the big party --- where can we get the liquor, etc.

I don't know why I write you so many letters. You never write me nuthin', and when you do it's only to yell at me for not writing you nuthin'.

It's playing pretty music on the radio. You're pretty too, only you never write me no letters. Why? I don't know why I should still love you, but I do I guess. Dammit.

***

Monday, Nov. 20, 1944

Luxembourg

Dear *(sister-in-law)* Rivkie:

It's typical California weather --- raining like hell. But do you think

206

I'm wet? Hell no. I'm sitting in the lobby of a classy hotel in a summer resort town. And at night I sleep between sheets. Such are the fortunes of war --- they range all the way from a muddy foxhole to a private room in a hotel. I'm not on leave either. My whole outfit is living this way now. In fact, we're having two dances this week --- one Regimental and one Battalion dance. The last dance we had was back in Angers (a very nice city in France). We haven't done any real heavy fighting since we took St. Malo and Dinard. The time we put in on the line here was in a very quiet sector. I haven't seen a dead German in more than two weeks. He was a man of 40, with gray hair, and had come to visit our lines on patrol. One of our boys neatly clipped off the top of his scalp with an M-1 rifle bullet. They let the patrol get to within about 20 yards, and then this one soldier drilled both the patrol leader and assistant patrol leader through the head. Both Krauts were armed with sub-machine guns, but they never got to fire a shot. We didn't find the older man's body till morning. The Colonel gave the soldier who had done the shooting his last bottle of Scotch. It's a fine state of affairs we've arrived at when people get rewarded just for killing Germans.

Last night the hotel owner's wife and the two maids decided to play a practical joke on me and the other officer in my room. They short-sheeted us, and stood waiting outside our room, giggling, and listening to hear us swear when we tried to climb into bed. But we disappointed them --- three years in the Army is too long to have spent without learning how to handle a short-sheet. I just pulled out a pair of scissors and cut holes for my legs to go through and went to sleep. Then they called up on the phone, still laughing, "Oh, monsieur, are you sleeping well tonight?"

Luxembourg is a pretty fine country. There were a lot of collaborators, but they either left with the Germans or are in jail now. The rest of the people hate the Germans' guts. When Germany annexed this area they promised that the Luxembourgers would never have to fight in the German Army. But when the German Army was being cut down to size on the Russian front, they declared a conscription of all Luxembourgers from 18 to 24. All those who ran away or hid out had their entire family arrested and sent to Germany in slavery. The entire country then went on strike, upon which the Germans declared all the strikers hostages, and proceeded to shoot a new group every day until they broke the strike. But the local militia continued its resistance movement, the same way as in France. The people are particularly indignant about the treatment of the Jews --- there were 2,000 of them here. The population of the whole Duchy is about 300,000. The standard of living is fairly good. The people look healthy, although the girls aren't anywheres near as pretty as in France. But every farm and every village has electricity and running water, two things which are non-existent in France, except in the large cities.

They have their own Luxembourg dialect, which is a sort of mixture of German and French, with a lot of words that sound like Yiddish. However, every man, woman, and child speaks German, so I've had no language difficulties like in France. My German has reached the point where I can speak quite easily, but my Russian has deteriorated somewhat recently. Anyway, about 85% of the people here speak French, and about 15% or 20% know some English. Languages are stressed in the schools, and they start studying languages in the primary grades.

If only the weather would stop being so crumby maybe the war would end. This way it's dragging out too much. However, be a good dopey kid. So long, Rivkie.

***

Sunday, Nov. 26, 1944

Luxembourg

Dear Dopey:

Same story. No mail.

No more clean sheets and fancy hotel. Back to the cowflop. It's very annoying. I got so used to sinks and toilets and beds.

The civilians in this little town invited all the soldiers to all three meals today, in commemoration of our Thanksgiving. I had dinner at some family's house, together with a couple of other officers. I had each course about three times, so that means I've had two Thanksgiving dinners --- one was the G.I. one last Thursday, and the second was this one. I practically ate myself to death. And filled up on wine and schnapps.

When we first arrived in Luxembourg everybody was saying, "You can see the difference here --- it's not like in France --- these people are pro-German." But the fellows soon learned different. These people aren't as demonstrative as the French. They don't make V-signs with their fingers, or run out and kiss you. But the feeling is the same. They fight with each other for the privilege of billeting soldiers in their houses. "You had three soldiers in your house all week," they say to their neighbors. "This time it's my turn." When they can't find soldiers who will live with them they feel slighted. Anyway, today every family in town invited several soldiers to each meal. They all say the same thing, "You don't know how long we waited for you."

The people I had dinner with took pictures of us all together with the family. If I'm still here when the pictures have been developed, I'll send you one or two maybe, if you're not still so mad at me that you don't care if you never see me again.

Gee, I miss you so much tonight. If you only knew.

***

Monday, Nov. 27, 1944

Luxembourg

Dear Baby:

The mail broke through today with the fastest service yet --- seven days. There should be a whole stack of letters coming, since there's a gap between Nov. 6 and Nov. 19. I'm glad you finally understand that I was just letting off steam in those other letters.

For the first time, I believe, since I've been overseas, my father actually wrote me a letter. It's always my mother who writes. He wrote a very good letter. It is obvious that he put a lot of time in on it and made free use of a dictionary. In spite of occasional mistakes in spelling, it's a remarkably well written letter for a man of his background. He certainly has a flair for writing which you wouldn't suspect from his speech. He says, "Your extremely careless handwriting and somewhat capricious remarks made us think that not everything is well with you, though we attributed most of it to the situation in which you were once before and are now again. ... You are anxious to know more about us. What is there to tell? That we are alive you can see from every letter of ours. Otherwise everything is almost as it was. Our life, as you know, was always a hard one, but we somehow pull through. ... A war before this one, pogroms, revolution, civil war, famine, etc., etc. Then America --- new country, new language, new surroundings, new ways of making a living. Struggle, struggle, and struggle. Then for a while came imaginary prosperity, and after that still more and more struggle."

I sure feel a lot better after today's batch of letters. Don't worry about me. I'm still in a pretty quiet spot, --- and even if it should get hot, it'll never be like those hedgerows. Nobody can imagine what those hedgerows were. There sure are a lot of boys who never got past them.

We're having another dance --- a Regimental dance, over in the big town. So you can see that we can't be doing such hard fighting if we can hold a dance in the middle of the war. A lot of the outfits who are making the offensives are pretty fresh ones, who never had to go through those hedgerows. Our reserves certainly seem to be endless. I don't think the Germans actually imagine how much we have got. There are so many outfits all over Europe who are just sitting and waiting to be thrown in if they are actually needed, while the Germans are really scraping bottom. Anyway, only 50% of the officers can go to the dance since after all we are on line. The Germans can't ever seem to hit anybody with their Artillery over here. We just sit and laugh when we hear incoming mail. It seems so petty and feeble compared to what that SS outfit we ran into in Normandy had to dish out.

My life isn't hard at all, dopey, but very boring. I sure wish I knew how much longer we've got to go.

The Colonel won a hundred francs off me. He said, "The wages of sin is death," and I said it's "are death." So we asked the Chaplain and looked it up in the Bible. But I haven't got a hundred francs. However, I really break even, because I found someone dumb enough to bet on Dewey, and he owes me a hundred. Everybody plays poker every night but me.

Why do those silly Nazis build fires right on the front lines and get themselves killed by our Artillery? They give me such a pain --- the schlemiels should have given up long ago. They're wasting my time. I hope they all get killed.

Goodnite, miss dopey. I love you.

***

V-mail: Friday nite, Nov. 29, 1944

Luxembourg

Dear Dopey:

No mail again, dammit. Rain, rain, rain. Was over to Germany to look the situation over. The main street of a town is called *Adolf Hitler Strasse,* and the civilians just stand and look at you. About two or three miles behind the front lines stood the inevitable Clubmobile, and the Red Cross girl doling out doughnuts to the G.I.'s. Kept on going, and messed around the forward position for a while, until a German machine gun went burp-burp! and the bullets kicked up dirt near my feet --- and I had seen enough, so I went home. Why does it have to keep raining all the time? The war would be over if it weren't for the damn weather. The rain can't last forever. So long, baby-face.

***

Thursday, Nov. 30, 1944

Luxembourg

Dear Dopey:

The pictures I have enclosed are quite recent --- they were taken only a few days ago. The tall lanky guy with the close-cropped blonde hair is the boss --- Lt. Col. John A. Norris, 29 years old, West Point Class of '38. The one with the pipe is our present Bn. Executive Officer, Capt. Calhoun, and the one who looks like a gorilla, with a shock of black hair, is Schmitt, the S-3. The tall thin one without a jacket on is Perrigo, the Operations Sgt. You know who the other gink is --- you married him.

I feel groggy as anything. We had our Regimental dance last night, and didn't get back until 0200 in the morning, and because of something that came up, I didn't get to sleep until after three, and I had to get up around six, so that's why I feel so groggy. Ever since the mail started arriving I've been getting a letter from you and from my parents every day. But every day it's an older letter. It's a funny sequence, like reading a book backwards, but at least I'm finding out what was going on. You were figuring out where I was in terms of the Third Army, and I've been in the First for months.

Oh, yes, the dance. It was very good. Everybody got slightly drunk, and some not so slightly. I was my usual slightly tipsy happy shicker --- the Colonel about the same. Calhoun got loaded, and went back to the car and went out cold. So did the Artillery liaison officer. Liquor flowed freely --- the girls were pretty as Luxembourg girls go --- more so than at the small town where we had the dance last week. This was the big city, and everything was very nice. We all had a swell time. I like parties. After the war we will have lots of parties. Everybody is so happy. Me too.

I can really operate at these parties --- not many officers speak German. The prettiest girl there came with a full-chicken Colonel, who commands another Regiment of the Division. He is a very nice young guy, and comes from the same class at West Point as Col. Norris.

Anyway, this babe was pretty nice, and she danced like American girls, not in the clumsy way most of these girls have.

"I am astonished," she said, "at the way you speak German. Never have I encountered an American who can speak such good German, and who waltzes so well."

"You are very beautiful," I said. "You are the most beautiful Mädchen in this entire ballroom."

"Oh, no," she said.

"Oh, yes," I said.

"Will you come and visit me when you are in Luxembourg again?" she asked.

"But certainly," I said, and took her address. But alack and alas, I am afraid I shall not see Luxembourg city again. That period is ended. The war has passed it by.

But it's a nice country, is Luxembourg. Every time the people see our soldiers moving out, they say, "Why are you leaving us? Have you found a better house to stay in?" Our soldiers insist that the house is fine, but they have to leave anyway. "Maybe your bed is not comfortable enough," the people say. "Take my bed." And every time we leave they are sad. "You will come back, won't you?"

I must go to sleep now. Why don't you send me pictures? I always send you pictures, and you never reciprocate.

***

10 GERMANY

Vacation was over. It was back to the killing fields again. We relieved the 4th Division in Hürtgen forest, where they had been cut to pieces. It was the deepest penetration of the Siegfried line at the time.

One night a prisoner came through to us, and told an amazing story. The German high command, he said, was planning a major offensive with massed troops and armor. He seemed to know the approximate date, and showed on the map where the breakthrough would come --- in the vicinity of Ardennes forest and Bastogne --- and where tanks were being massed. I called Regiment immediately, and around midnight sent him on a jeep back to where interrogation teams were waiting. The next morning they called and asked what I thought of the prisoner's credibility.

"What do I know about his credibility?" I said.

"We find his story hard to believe," they said. "He claims he's been in the Army only a couple of weeks, yet he knows how to read a map. And how would a Private soldier have access to all this information?"

V-mail: Dec. 4, 1944

Germany

Dear Dopey Darling:

I'm afraid my letters will have to be much less frequent now. Back to work again. You will observe that there has been a radical change of address. It won't be long now. The Siegfried line is behind us, and it will take only one more good push.

We're living in holes again, and it's been raining constantly. I took off my shoes last night and got into my sack, and managed to keep dry. But in the morning my shoes were full of water. So I dumped out the water and wiped my shoes dry with my handkerchief. My feet are still dry, since I wear my overshoes all the time. It was rather hard getting back into real combat again, and we were all feeling pretty low. In fact I didn't eat for a couple of days. This morning I forced myself to eat, and I feel a million times better. I've adjusted myself again. In fact, I'm hungry as hell, so I know I'm back to normal. If those damn Krauts drop any shells in the middle of this letter I will be very angry.

How are you, sweetheart? I love you very much. Don't worry about me. I'm feeling chipper again. But don't mind if I don't get a chance to write much. You'd be surprised at the obstacles. Be home soon maybe. Love, dopey.

***

Dec. 8, 1944

Germany

Dear Dopey:

I am sending you the negatives of the pictures I sent you before. I think it's very something-or-other that I've sent you so many pictures and you have only sent me one little old one that wasn't much good. I got a whole slew of mail from you yesterday, and they say there's more mail today.

215

Writing conditions are rather inconducive here. I'm in a dugout the Krauts built for us. It's around five feet deep, and covered with a roof of shellproof (?) logs. There are around ten or twelve people in here and you can't even move an elbow without running your face into somebody's muddy foot. I have to use a flashlight because it's so dark in here. This is the nearest thing to the pictures of World War I I've seen. Of course the sun is out, and it's a nice clear day for a change, but I know that as soon as I step out and start writing outside, those stinkers will lob some shells over, and I'll only have to dive for the hole again, so what's the percentage. It's bad enough when a man even has to answer the calls of nature.

However, I'm feeling real fine. Yesterday I did something rather remarkable. I took a shave and a shower. Really. There was an opportunity to go back to Service Company for a hot shower, which I did --- not because I felt like bathing, but because I figured it was a good idea. There's nothing particularly appealing about a bath when you only have to crawl back into the same mud again, but what the hell. I was amazed when I looked in a mirror at myself. You wouldn't recognize me. I had the longest beard I've ever seen on my face yet. But I look real pretty now.

How about you? I bet you look real pretty too, miss dopey.

I didn't kid Irv much in the letter I wrote him, but I thought he belonged to a demonstration outfit stationed at the Infantry School, or something. You can't blame people for talking like that sometimes. Everybody does it. The lead scout of a platoon thinks the soldiers behind him have it soft, and they in turn believe the Company Hq has a racket, and the latter think the same of Battalion, who says the same of Regiment, and so on back. And they're all perfectly right. It's completely relative. You know how the G.I.'s here feel about the guys still back in the States.

Anyway, Reg't S-3 is a damn good job. It's a desk job fundamentally, even under field conditions (I'm speaking relatively, of course), but it's a very important tactical job, and gives a man pretty good experience.

(I got tired of that stinking hole, so I've come out in the sun to finish the letter.)

How's Carl? Will he regain the use of his leg completely?

You're very silly, dopey, to work such long hours. You can get just as much experience without all that overtime. As for the money, what good is money? The only thing important is to be alive and enjoy it.

It's too bad about your mother bothering Rivkie. That's terrible. But after all, parents have to have some fun too, and that's their form of recreation.

Keep writing me nice letters.

Two soldiers in my outfit got picked to go home on the rotation plan. They thought everybody who told them about it was crazy. At first we couldn't find one of the guys, and we thought maybe he was dead or something, but he turned up in some hole. Imagine being whisked up out of all this and being deposited in Times Square. Wow.

Oh, yes, keep sending me things to eat. Anything is handy now --- preferably small packages. Cocoa, candy, cookies, canned chicken or meat, or anything in fact, will be appreciated by all concerned.

Love, you darling dopey kid. See you soon, I hope.

***

V-mail: Sat'y, Dec. 9, 1944

Germany

Dear Dopey:

I'm getting off a fast dehydrated letter while I've got a chance to mail it. I got your letter of Nov. 29 today, in which you sound so much more cheerful, having received a lot of letters. Anything at all involving home sounds ridiculously cheerful. It doesn't matter whether it involves work or vacation or school. Haven't you gotten any of the pictures I sent you? You don't mention any of them.

How are you, pieface darling? It's nice to get your pretty pink letters. Where did you get that fancy stationary? You still haven't told me. We spend what leisure time we get telling silly stories, reminiscing, or betting when the war will end.

Love, dopey.

***

The next day before dawn we attacked. It had just begun to snow. The Germans had no shortage of ammunition, and the shelling was the heaviest I had ever encountered, worse even than Normandy. In the days that followed the familiar smell of death was everywhere. (I never did find out the source of that smell, --- whether it was the cordite in the high explosives or the decaying bodies.)

Our planes were grounded by poor visibility, and for the first time the Luftwaffe appeared. The Messerschmidt came in low, skimming the tree tops. Even before I could see or hear the plane, streams of bullets cracked past, kicking up the ground on both sides of me. Then the plane passed over, and there was no place to hide, only waiting helplessly to see if it would return for another pass.

The most vivid image is of a long narrow ditch that had to be traversed repeatedly between Battalion and Company. It was used because the shelling would not allow anyone to survive long above ground. But this meant having to step over the dead and the dying who lined the ditch, mainly Germans. Those still living would recoil, afraid their faces would be stepped on. I could recognize among the dead some who had been alive on earlier trips. Our wounded had to be evacuated on litters either along the same ditch, which would have been very difficult, or else above ground amidst the shelling. The Company Commander asked me if I would help carry one of the litters, and it is on my conscience to this very day that I refused him, choosing to say I could not take the time.

Finally we seized the ruins of a little village called Strass, and could go no further. The only overhead shelter remaining intact was a single cellar adjacent to a courtyard, and there we established the Battalion O.P. The Germans knew exactly where we were, because they had just been there themselves, and their mortars were zeroed in. We were a salient with the enemy on three sides, and the fourth side was fully exposed to enemy fire and observation. Nothing could get in or out in the daytime without being shot up. A doctor infiltrated through during the night, but he had no medicine. The wounded were dying, we were practically out of ammunition, and the only water available was that in the streets. I remember filling my canteen from the gutter and not bothering with the sterilizing pills everyone carried. What difference did it make, if you were likely to be dead soon anyway.

The Regimental Commander had apparently been hit, and a new one without combat experience took over, fresh from Benning. He sent us a radio message with the School Solution. "You won't believe this," I said, handing it to the Colonel. It said, "The best way to remedy your situation is by taking aggressive action."

On Dec. 14 a platoon of tanks tried to run the gauntlet with water and ammunition, but they never made it, except for the ones who managed to reach us after escaping from their disabled tanks alive. We had a couple of dozen prisoners, including an Oberleutnant who demanded they be evacuated at once. The shelling was so heavy they would all be killed, and it was against the Geneva Convention. "How can I evacuate you?" I said. He claimed the Germans would not fire on their own people. That was when I got the idea that the prisoners could carry the wounded, the tankers would guard the prisoners, and maybe they would all make it back.

While I was standing in the courtyard explaining this plan to the tankers, someone brought up two new prisoners, whom I started to interrogate briefly. The next thing that happened, as if a string had suddenly been cut, was an abrupt loss of consciousness. When it returned I was lying on the ground with legs ringing from concussion and a mortar barrage still coming down, --- heavy stuff, probably 120 mm. I was sure I had lost both legs and was dying. From somewhere came the sound of my own voice crying for help. I could raise my head slightly, which made it possible to see that the legs were still attached. But the right arm would not move, and I thought it had been blown off. Then I realized I could wiggle my fingers.

When the barrage lifted, people came out of the cellar and put me on a litter. But I could see that everyone else in the courtyard was dead, all of the tankers as well as the two prisoners. Back in the cellar a medic cut away the field jacket, sprinkled sulfa and bound my right shoulder, which was wide open. I could not move my body.

The Colonel came to say goodbye. "What's the idea of getting hit, Baker?" he asked me.

"I don't know, Colonel," I said. "I guess I just ---- up."

I passed out again.

Then the Regiment on our left broke through and ambulances were able to come up. I remember waking and seeing the Chaplain looking down at me. Before long I was in a field hospital in Aachen, lying in a nice clean bed, knowing I still had all my limbs and most everything else. But I kept having nightmares and "daymares" in which I found myself walking along that same ditch, stepping over the same bodies. It was the one time in my life in which I genuinely wanted to be dead. But death never came.

***

5 days later.

V-Mail: Dec. 19, 1944

(In another handwriting) Germany

Dear Dora:

I just found out that I am not supposed to write about the nature of my wounds, which I did in my last two letters. So if they come thru blackened out, don't let it worry you too much. I'm feeling fine, although they tell me that I have one of those million dollar wounds that will probably have me sent back to the States eventually. However, don't base any plans on my quick return, because it may take months. Don't mind my letters sounding like a business letter. It's still too hard for me to write myself, so I have to dictate them. I never thought I would have to spend Christmas flat on my back, but it could have been much worse. At least we know there will be nothing missing next Christmas.

Love to everyone.

***

V-Mail: Dec. 21, 1944

Germany

(In my own, but very shaky, handwriting)

Dear Dopey face:

Been flat on my back a week now and it's very boring. But there's nothing I can do about it. I guess if I could take the combat part of it I can take this too. I am getting well enough to sit on the side of my bed now.

Not hearing from you doesn't help any either. I won't get any mail forwarded to me till I get to the General Hospital, and I don't know how long I'll have to wait after that. But keep on writing. It will get to me eventually. How are you, baby? I wish I knew what you're doing.

Your grandma must have put in a right tall job of praying for me, dopey. I guess she got me a special dispensation. The other seven boys hit by the same shell were beyond medical care when the smoke had cleared away.

It's very hard to write, because my arm is strapped to my side. So don't worry if you don't get letters often. Explain same to my folks. I'm really getting well fast.

Love, dopey darling.

***

It took a month to get to England from the field hospital in Aachen where the first surgery was done. The ambulance drove through a forest, probably the Ardennes. The driver was nervous because there was news that German armor had just broken through. "I sure hope we make it without being caught by German tanks," he said.

One night there was a stop in which prisoners were being used to carry the litters around to a rear entrance where there was some sort of makeshift hospital. They marched in lock step, so that the litter bounced up and down. It was pitch dark, and one of them said to the other, "You know, if we dropped this bird in the ditch over there, no one would ever notice." I was infuriated and about to let them know I understood German and was an officer, but I was flat on my back in a body cast and totally helpless. They evidently thought better of it also.

When the ambulance arrived in Liege the next day, the city was being buzz-bombed. Every few minutes a V-1 could be heard coming in, and after the engine shut off there was the terrifying wait for the explosion that followed. But even under these conditions the doctors performed surgery on my shoulder.

More surgery took place at a hospital in Paris, a city that had to be viewed through the window of an ambulance. The bad news was I had developed a rash which they diagnosed as measles, and I was confined to an isolation ward in which the patient on one side had spinal meningitis, and on the other side tuberculosis. For a chest case this seemed like madness, and I raised a howl of complaint, after which they decided to call it a reaction to sulfa drugs and removed me from the isolation ward.

There was still more surgery in Cherbourg, and then it was back across the channel to the long-term destination, an Army hospital in England near the Welsh border. There appear to be no letters written during this entire period.

11 ENGLAND

It was called Hospital Plant 4189, and was the chest center of the European Theatre. Everybody was a chest case. But the amazing thing that struck me is that they had all been wounded on the right side. Now why should that be? What was the cause of this strange asymmetry? Was there something about always hitting the ground with the rifle in firing position on the right side, so that it was always the right side of the body that was exposed to enemy fire? Or was the Army systematically dividing up the cases, so that somewhere else in the European Theatre there was another Hospital Plant with all the left-handed chest wounds? This did not seem to make much sense, despite the Army's well known preoccupation with classification and orderliness.

It took me a few days to solve the riddle. The answer was so obvious. Everyone who had been hit on the left side was dead.

***

(In another handwriting)   21 January, 1945

England

Dear Dora:

My invasion in reverse is proceeding according to plan, however slowly. They tell me that I will probably be home sometime in March, but don't depend on it. It took me over a month to get to England, where it would have taken only a little over an hour by air evacuation, which I thought I would get.

I've landed in a hospital which is a chest center, specializing in chest cases. They have a Lt. Col. here who is one of the top men in the field. I'm still carrying a souvenir from the Krupp works in my chest which he's going to remove in a few days. They have their own policy here regarding the treatment of chest cases. In the other hospitals where I've been they told me that I wouldn't be able to move around much for several months, but here they take the very opposite point of view. For the last two days I've been learning to walk again after spending over a month in bed, so by the time I get home I guess I'll be pretty spry again, and I sure can't wait to get home. You understand of course that if I get into Halloran General Hospital at Staten Island I will expect you to bring me stuff to eat every day.

Incidentally, you are now married to a man with only nine toes, since one of them is missing in action somewhere in Germany. I only found out about it a month after I was hit, when my foot had healed and they took the bandage off. I stuck my foot up in the air and could only count four toes, whereas I am almost positive that I had five when I left the States. It is the next to the last toe on the right foot, and was never of any use to anybody anyway. It was blown off by the concussion, and the amazing thing about it was that neither my shoe nor my overshoe showed any tear or hole or other sign of damage. So there is a physics problem for you to do research on.

I am feeling swell, especially now that I can move around and there's no pain or discomfort of any kind any more, although of course my shoulder is still in a cast. Just after I was hit I had no appetite at all for a couple of weeks, but now I am back to normal again, which means you'd better get my mother to start cooking for me right away.

It's a nice feeling to know that I'll spend this spring with you. It's been a long time since I've been able to plan ahead like that, or even be reasonably sure I'd be alive at any time in the future. Don't be surprised at the tone of my letters or the infrequency. I just can't get enough movement out of my right hand, because of the cast, to write them myself. Why worry about letters when I'll be there in a flash before long, except for that one ridiculous toe that's missing in action.

Everybody here is all excited about the Russian drive. I guess they are sort of banking on the war's being over before they get back to duty. The battle cry here is, "Go, Russians, go!"

So long, kid. Just a little longer for us to sweat out now. Love to everybody.

***

(In my own handwriting)   Sunday, Feb. 4, 1945

England

Dear Dopey darling:

You've liberated me this morning. There must be something to this business of psychological curing. Today I received my first mail --- a little V-mail from you, and behold, my spirits are so elevated that I've found enough strength in my bum right arm to write again. Dopey, you have no idea how wonderful I feel. I really believe I will get well fast now. Until today I've been feeling pretty low. I've just come through two operations --- one on my shoulder, to cut away infected tissue and obtain secondary closure on the big ugly wound I had there. You could almost stick your fist in it down to the bone. I once made the mistake of looking at it while they were changing the dressing, and I got sick and nearly passed out --- and after all I've seen. But it's all closed up now. They took the stitches out yesterday. Anyway, three days later, before I fully recovered, they wheeled me back into the operation room, and did a major operation on my chest to remove a big jagged piece of iron three inches long. Wait till I show it to you. One end was in my right lung and the other end was close to my heart.

> *The worst part of the chest surgery was in the days that followed. Rubber tubes had been inserted to allow for drainage. Every morning a team of doctors would start at one end of the long recovery room, pushing a little cart with a syringe to clear the tubes using penicillin under pressure. Each patient waited his turn, and the closer the team approached, the louder became the sounds of the screaming. Fortunately this procedure lasted only a few days.*

You don't know how lucky we are, dopey. If this were the last war it would have been curtains for me. My life was saved by modern surgery, penicillin, and sulfa drugs. I took the latter within one minute after I was wounded, and received the first operation on my chest only a few hours later at the evacuation hospital. If I had been wounded a day or two earlier I would probably have died. Here's what happened. I was standing in a courtyard in a battered little German town. We had reached the town during the night a couple of days previously by moving across country at night. The Germans held all our roads to the rear, and all the terrain around us was under fire. We had no way of getting food, water, and ammunition up to us. And worse yet, there was no way of evacuating the wounded. The day I was hit a general attack had begun again. I was questioning a prisoner, and there were seven men bunched around, as they had no business to be. A mortar shell (81 mm.) landed right on us, wounding me and killing the other seven men. Just about that time the roads were cleared and the attack went forward. So very shortly afterwards ambulances came right up and picked up all the wounded.

Anyway, I hope I'm through with operations now. I'm up and walking around. The policy here is that every patient has to get up and walk the very day after his operation. It's agony, but it keeps you from becoming an invalid, and you start expanding your lungs right away. Anyway, my operation was around five days ago, and I really get around now. I hardly stay in bed at all in the day time.

My right arm has been in a sling for the last couple of weeks instead of the cast, so they could work on me.

But I'm afraid you wouldn't recognize me now, dopey. You've been gypped. I'm just not the big healthy guy you married. I weigh 138 lbs. You probably can't believe that. But a chest wound does that to a man. It will take many months to get back to my former self, but we'll do it. I suspect that I won't be back to the States by March. I think it'll probably be in April. You see, before they'll let me go my chest has to be expanded again, and I have to be well on the way to recovery. Then I'll have to start waiting my turn for space on a hospital ship. Anyway, dopey, we can wait a little longer if necessary. They won't do any work on my shoulder here. Anyway, I figure that we'll spend at least a month or so at some place in the country this summer, where I can pick up some sunshine and health. The hospital back home will be giving me plenty of leave, I'm certain. Incidentally, I'll never regain full use of my right arm. The movement of the forearm and hand are not affected, and I will have complete movement there. But a piece of the upper part of the humerus was completely shot out, so that I will never have 100% movement of my upper arm. Lt. Col. Miscell, who did both operations on me here, and is the top chest surgeon in this theatre, believes that scar tissue will fill the gap, and that's how the movement will be restored. I'll probably be able to raise my elbow to the height of my shoulder, but no higher. So you can see it will be no real handicap.

No, I won't be sent to Carl's hospital. Fortunately all my nerves and blood vessels completely escaped injury. It always surprises the doctors when they see me for the first time. In most wounds like mine the nerve is also affected, and the arm and hand are paralyzed. But my lucky star worked again. It's a wonder I didn't lose the arm altogether.

I'm out of the Army though, I believe, as soon as they finish working on me back in the States, unless I'm willing to accept limited service, which doesn't appeal to me particularly.

A guy named Saul Wellman, who used to command the MacKenzie-Papinou Bn. in Spain, is a patient in my ward now. They took a piece of metal out of his heart. He was a Corporal in the Paratroops.

I'm sending you another 2,000 ice cream cones worth of money.

My arm is getting awfully tired, sweetheart. But you'll hear much more often now. You can tell my parents as much about my condition as you think wise. I'm not writing them any details. I leave that up to you.

So long, pieface. Your skinny husband.

EPILOGUE

The phone call came in April, just about a year after I had left. In no time at all she was on the train bound for Newport News, Virginia. I had come home on an American hospital ship that for the most part carried wounded Infantrymen and rotated Air Corps fliers.

It was the happiest week of my life. The food was wonderful, the same for both officers and enlisted men. Actually I had been scheduled to go sooner, but the wounds became infected again, and the trip had to be postponed. "We wash our own dirty linens here," Miscell told me. The result was that, whereas the original orders said litter case, by the time I went I was completely ambulatory. But the mills of the gods grind slow. The Army had me typed as a litter case, and so it had to be.

When I entered a railway car assigned to me and saw that everybody was on litters, I said to the officer in charge, "It's a mistake. I'm no longer a litter case."

"Let me see your orders," he said. Then, looking back up at me, "Sure, you're no litter case. No litter case. Just lie down over there."

When I tried to board ship and explained the whole story to the medical officer at the gangplank, he said, "Look, they know what they're doing back there. If they classified you a litter case, they must have had their reasons. Besides, everybody is counting heads, and if the number of litter cases and ambulatory cases doesn't check out, nobody goes." So I had to lie down and be carried aboard by four husky G.I.'s, after which I thanked them and walked off. The same procedure was followed in reverse at Newport News, where I checked in at the receiving hospital.

She walked through the ward looking for me, and seeing all the wreckage of war. Everybody was laughing and kidding around. When I saw her I pulled my right arm out of the sling and we threw our arms around each other, although one of mine could not squeeze very hard. At the other end of the ward a group of patients were tossing a multiple amputee back and forth between two blankets, and all of them laughing uproariously, as if the whole thing had been some kind of big joke or game, in which they were the winners.

Figure 1: A piece of shrapnel removed from Adolph's chest.

Figure 2: Adolph's Purple Heart and Bronze Star medals.

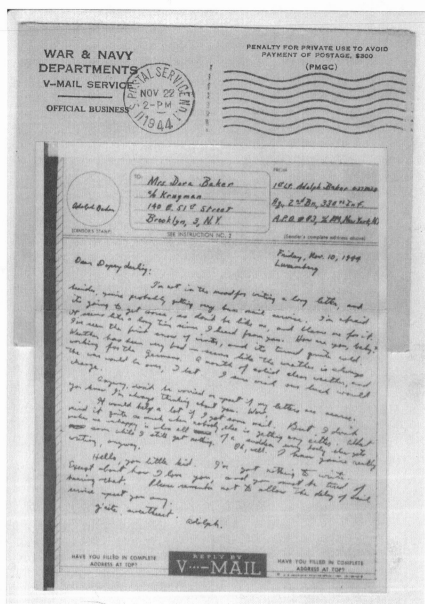

Figure 3: An image of the V-mail Adolph sent to Dora on Nov. 10, 1944. He omitted the content of this letter from the manuscript.

Figure 4: A photo of Dora.

Figure 5: A photo of Adolph in uniform.

20578680R00149

Made in the USA
Charleston, SC
18 July 2013